1989

A BROADCAST NEWS MANUAL OF STYLE

Developed under the advisory editorship of
Thomas W. Bohn, Dean School of Communications, Ithaca
College

A BROADCAST NEWS MANUAL OF STYLE

R. H. MacDONALD
Washington and Lee University

Longman
New York & London

Executive Editor: Gordon T. R. Anderson
Production Editor: Helen B. Ambrosio
Text Design: Angela Foote
Cover Design: Joseph DePinho
Production Supervisor: Eduardo Castillo
Compositor: Best-Set Typesetter Ltd.
Printer and Binder: Maple-Vail Book Manufacturing Group

A Broadcast News Manual of Style

Longman Inc.
95 Church Street
White Plains, N.Y. 10601

Associated companies:
Longman Group Ltd., London
Longman Cheshire Pty., Melbourne
Longman Paul Pty., Auckland
Copp Clark Pitman, Toronto
Pitman Publishing Inc., New York

Library of Congress Cataloging-in-Publication Data

MacDonald, R. H., 1932–
 A broadcast news manual of style.

 Bibliography: p.
 Includes index.
 1. Broadcast journalism—Authorship. 2. Journalism—
Style manuals. I. Title.
PN4784.B75M24   1987   808'.02   86-27463
ISBN 0-582-99865-4

88 89 90 9 8 7 6 5 4 3 2

CONTENTS

INTRODUCTION

To my knowledge, there is no extensive style, format and usage guide for broadcast newswriters. To be sure, there are numerous textbooks on broadcast newswriting and most of them contain usage and style guides. But, those guides are usually brief or narrow in scope or both. There are many good English usage guides available but none that directly addresses the needs of the broadcaster. Broadcast newswriting needs to be precise and unmistakably clear. Careful use of the language is essential to that process. This book, therefore, is presented primarily as a usage guide, although one will find sections on "style," page formats, punctuation, editing and the more mechanical aspects of getting words on paper.

Many newsrooms rely on the usage guides published by The Associated Press (AP) or the United Press International (UPI) (they are very similar). Those, however, were written for people who work for the wire services and therefore tend to perpetuate the peculiarities of wire service style and usage. An example is their refusal to recognize *persons* as a plural of *person*, insisting instead that *people* must be used in every case. That is simply not precise. This is not to say the AP or UPI usage guides are poor. They are, in fact, excellent in most cases and every good newsroom should have one or the other. However, they were adapted partly from style and usage guides that were developed for the newspaper wires, for which a different approach to newswriting is recommended.

The AP Broadcast News Handbook, for example, contains the AP's preferred spellings and hyphenation techniques as well as numerous entries detailing the correct names and headquarter cities of major airlines and other companies and the rules of a variety of sporting events and games. That information is handy

1

for someone writing to the standardized style of the AP, but is extra baggage for the broadcast newswriter working for a local audience. A smaller, less cluttered usage guide, would be preferred.

Most broadcast newswriting texts deal with writing style, not good writing. They tend to concentrate on snappy leads, too brief storytelling and writing to video. That's all good, but sometimes a story needs more serious treatment, longer exposition and complete sentences. Texts also seem to dwell in more than necessary detail on reporting techniques (which should have been taught in Reporting 101, not in a broadcast newswriting class at the advanced level) and mechanical skills, such as tape editing.

What the reader will find here are discussions of what we're calling "style" for want of a better word. Style here includes the more mechanical aspects of newswriting—page formats, how to cue tapes, etc—for both radio and television. It must be understood that these are examples of one way to construct script pages. There are nearly 15,000 radio and TV stations in this country and perhaps dozens of different ways of formatting a page. What is presented here is conventional enough to be acceptable in most places. But anyone contemplating working in any newsroom must be ready to adapt to its way of doing things. Areas of difference or disagreement have been noted. The use (or nonuse) of contractions is an example. Some texts urge the writer to use lots of contractions; I do not. A discussion of that disagreement can be found in the section on writing.

When I entered television news in its infancy, there were no "right" or "wrong" ways to do things. Newswriters learned by experimenting. Most newsrooms in the mid-1950s developed independently. Consequently, many different methods of handling copy and conventions of usage emerged. What you will find here is the evolved result of my own experimenting, now augmented by the experience of others as contained in many textbooks. The result is a set of "rules" that may differ in detail from those presented in some texts. However, the intent and, I hope, the result will be similar. Audience understanding and ease of copy handling are the goals. I believe the practices recommended here meet these goals. Classroom instructors and professionals who may use this guide are certainly free to adjust its recommendations to suit their preferred methods. Broadcast news is still an evolving craft. Each new piece of electronic magic that enters the newsroom has the potential of fundamentally changing present methods. The advent of portable video tape machines and electronic cameras has had profound effect. Future advancements certainly have the same potential. Rules evolve with the craft and change is inevitable.

As you read the following pages keep in mind that although things seem to be presented as commandments from on high, little in this business is cast in concrete (please note I did not say *cement*—see usage guide). Newsrooms have their little quirks and preferred ways of doing things. Every anchor has preferences as to how things ought to be done to suit his or her particular ways. And, in some cases, the methods change with circumstance. It is not considered a crime to break style for good reason. But to break style because of ignorance or carelessness is not easily forgiven. The writer who consistently misspells or ignores the conventions of page format is considered an unreliable coworker and a poor journalist.

Some of the conventions may seem unnecessary, but there is a reason for everything. Those reasons most often can be traced to the desire to help the listener understand. Some, however, are intended to help you and your colleagues do a better job. An example is the various ways numbers are handled in different circumstances. You will find, for instance, that the numbers one through eleven are usually spelled out in scripts while those numbers twelve and above are expressed as numerals. There are several exceptions to that rule, however. Many of the "rules" discussed have exceptions. The rules and exceptions are all intended to make the news and other information to be broadcast easier for the listener to comprehend. Listener understanding is, after all, most important.

Conventional style is extremely helpful in newsrooms with several writers working for the same news program. There would be chaos if the anchorperson was forced to wade through the differing styles, formats and spellings of several writers, each with his or her own rule book. It would be like moving from typewriter to typewriter, each with a different keyboard. If the anchor becomes confused, listener misunderstanding is sure to follow.

On another level, broadcasters have delivered news to the public for more than 50 years, and people are accustomed to hearing certain information presented in a certain format, which has developed to improve listener comprehension. The way routine weather forecasts are handled is an example.

Uniformity in newswriting is easier on the listener, on the

person who must read the copy on the air and on those who must work with the copy in preparing the news program.

Note the reference to the *news program*. I'm offended when our work is referred to as a *show*, and the word *newscast* is to my way of thinking, substandard English. *Newscast* is commonly used, however, and you'll find I use it, too.

Even though we're dealing with the spoken language, correct spelling remains of major importance. Misspellings will cause obvious problems for people reading someone else's writing aloud. In addition, problems of pronunciation and inflection arise when soundalike or look-alike words are misspelled. For example, to write *trusty* when you mean *trustee* can cause a great deal of embarrassment. Do doctors have *patients* or *patience* or both?

Be aware that regional idiom varies widely across the nation. A perfectly good expression in the mid-South might mean something entirely different in New England. An example is the noun variant for 18-wheel trucks. In the South and elsewhere they are called *tractor-trailers* (or, less commonly, *semis*, pronounced SEM-eyes). In Vermont they are called *trailer trucks*. If one used the phrase *tractor-trailer* in that farm-rich country, the image brought up would be that of a farm tractor pulling a hay wagon.

There are numerous examples of these regionalisms and quirks of usage that the newswriter must learn when settling into a new locality and attempting to communicate with its people.

Broadcast punctuation and how it differs from everyday use is discussed. The broadcast writer never writes anything that cannot be pronounced. Therefore, most of the symbols on the top row of your typewriter are useless. Everything to be said on the air must be written out in full. The broadcast writer will rarely use semicolons or colons. Instead, the copy will be sprinkled liberally with dashes--like that. Some writers will use the ellipsis (. . .) to do the same thing. I don't recommend it because it indicates that something has been left out of the text. Differing punctuation in broadcast newswriting is a purely mechanical thing. The divergence from "standard" punctuation is designed to help the copy reader. The differences should never be translated into formal writing. Most students of broadcast newswriting will spend most of their college careers in courses that demand correct, standard punctuation. Keep the specialized form presented here in the broadcast newsroom. Much nonstandard punctuation develops as the individual preference of the newsreader and is later formalized in a newsroom "stylebook." Such is what is presented here. The purpose is to aid the reader in smoothing delivery, looking for inflection traps, emphasizing key words and making a point. Used properly, nonstandard punctuation can go a long way toward the goals of clarity and comprehension.

The section on editing is brief, because there's not much to it. Generally, if a script page needs much editing, it should be re-written.

The usage guide that makes up the greater part of this book should be the most useful contribution. It is arranged alpha-betically with cross-references. One will find common words that are frequently either mispronounced or misused. One will also find my opinion as to which words are "better" for broadcast usage where there is a choice of two or more expressions. I would never, for example, use the word *practicable* in a broadcast news script, even though it is a perfectly good and useful word. I would substitute *practical* or *feasible* even though the meanings are slightly different. To be sure, other newswriters may use the word, but it is not easily pronounced or understood. Especially when writing for yourself to read on the air, beware of using words you are not comfortable with. They will trip you up every time. The usage guide also includes some lengthy discussions of the nomenclature of firearms and the jargon of weatherpersons, among other things. I have relied on *Webster's Ninth New Collegiate Dictionary* as my authority, even though it is more permissive than I like. It may come as a surprise to some that dictionaries frequently disagree, especially on matters of usage. And, there are some instances where Webster's Ninth and I do not agree. I have so noted.

Our language has been called the "glue of our society." It should be carefully protected—especially by those who make a living from its use.

There are some great writers working in broadcast news-rooms—but not many. For most, the pressures of hourly dead-lines and demands for ever-briefer stories make graceful and precise writing impossible. But those very pressures make precision necessary. When a newsreader has only a fraction of a minute to tell a complex story, precision of language—using the exact word to convey the precise thought—is essential.

But, before we can deal with the art of precision writing, we must deal with the mechanics. Every art, after all, begins as a craft. We must learn to execute the necessary moves before we can refine them into a graceful and pleasing result.

Many entries in the usage guide are not necessarily specific only to broadcast newswriting, but apply to all good writing. In many cases troublesome words are included with a suggestion that preference be given to words that are "better" for broadcasting, although there may be perfectly good substitutes. The preference is usually based on how the word sounds when spoken, but sometimes there are words that may confuse the anchor and lead to inflection problems.

In broadcast writing try to use conventional words—words listeners are accustomed to hearing and using in their daily lives. This does not mean we use coarse or crude language or slang, but it does mean that broadcast newswriting tends to be casual rather than formal.

Note there are several references to the way television weatherpersons mishandle the language. It may be some sort of misguided effort to be conversational or informal that leads to such nonsense phrases as "a widely scattered shower" or "the winds are presently calm."

No usage guide can ever be complete, unless it becomes a fully developed dictionary, and that's not what we're after here. I have relied on years of collecting misusages and mispronunciations that are commonly heard and seen, as well as on such excellent works as *Harper Dictionary of Contemporary Usage*, by William and Mary Morris, *The Writer's Art*, by James J. Kilpatrick, *A Treasury for Word Lovers*, by Morton Freeman and *Dictionary of Problem Words and Expressions*, by Harry Shaw. All are exhaustive, authoritative and witty examinations of our language. These are highly recommended for any writer's bookshelf.

One will find the inevitable appendixes at the end of the book. These contain standard patient condition definitions, the real meaning of "ten-four good buddy," a list of state capitals with pronouncers for the hard ones, a listing of the nations of the world and their capitals with pronouncers, telephone area codes by state and numerically, foreign telephone codes, codes of ethics, the FCC and the news, a discussion of libel and privacy and free press-fair trial guidelines.

The reader will find this a straightforward approach to the subject of broadcast newswriting practices. There is no attempt to make this a scholarly document. In fact, students of language and usage may very well take issue with some of the proclamations. That is one of the risks in writing about writing. There's always someone out there who's better at it and will find the little lapses and errors.

It is hoped the student of broadcast writing will find this a useful tool to supplement the excellent texts that are commonly used and that the practitioner will find this a useful reference.

My career has carried me from a start in radio in a town of 1,500 in Vermont to a major metropolitan area and finally to a smaller city where I spent the larger part of 18 professional years as a reporter, assignment editor, anchor and finally news director of the dominant television station. I have been teaching broadcast newswriting at the university level for 17 years. In 35 years I have seen or heard every one of the usage errors contained in this book—and many more.

I make no claim of being a grammarian or a linguist. I am merely a journalist who has spent my entire career working with words and shades of meaning and attempting, through precision of language, to make understandable the daily events of our times.

It was determined to write this book when frustration with existing guides reached an intolerable level. Student newswriting exercises and broadcast copy were so filled with errors that correcting and editing were taking a lot of time. The book began as a pamphlet distributed to students, which logically led to the idea of producing a real book to share with other instructors who may struggle with the mangled language of the average college student.

I have discussed the project with the author of a leading broadcast newswriting text and with several professional broadcast news directors whom I respect. All have given me strong encouragement.

STYLE AND FORMATS

9

The conventions of copy formats are by no means universal. Most newsrooms use similar rules for designing the different kinds of script pages, but the individual variations seem almost endless. Most have been developed through use and are almost traditional. What is presented here is a set of conventions that is widely accepted and would cause little problem. However, the reader must realize that when going to work in any newsroom, one must be ready to adapt to its way of doing things.

We will proceed on the assumption that the newsroom in which you find yourself is still using typewriters. There is a rapid move toward computerized broadcast newsrooms, in which case page formats will likely be decided automatically. Your first step, whether dealing with a typewriter or a computer terminal, is to become thoroughly familiar with the machine—infantile as it may seem. You must know how to set margins and tabular stops, how to change the ribbon and so on. Most students have great difficulty with unfamiliar typewriters. Get to be a friend of yours.

Page Design for Radio and Television

1.1 *Setting Margins and Tabular Stops for Radio Scripts*

A typical page of radio news copy is composed as follows:

First, set the paper guide on the top of the typewriter to zero. That's usually as far to the left as it will go. Then, set the first tabular stop at 10; we'll come back to this later. Set the left margin at 20 and another tab stop at 25. Still another tab stop should be set at 50 and the right margin at 80. This results in a 60-character line with a five-space indentation for paragraphs and a tab stop at midpage, which is useful for end marks and other purposes. This 60-character line takes the average newsreader 3 seconds, so 10 lines equal 30 seconds—making timing easy. Timing, of course depends on the newsreader. Some people simply read faster or slower than others.

1.2 *Setting Margins and Tabular Stops for Television Scripts*

A page of television news copy looks somewhat different from radio copy. The demands of television are so much greater than radio that more information needs to be put on the page—not to be read on the air but to tell the director and other production people what to do and when. In some TV newsrooms producers decide on visual effects and other such things, but often the writers are expected to turn in copy complete with all audio and video directions.

For a television news script, again set the paper guide at zero and a tab stop at 10, just as with radio. However, now we get into a quite different form. Set the left margin at 40 and the paragraph indent at 45; the mid-page tab stop is set at 60 and the right margin at 80. This gives us a 40-character line which takes about two seconds to read—still useful for timing as ten lines equal 20 seconds.

The extrawide left margin is used to write in video and audio directions. Some newsrooms provide copy paper that has a vertical ruling to set off the left margin. At Cable News Network (CNN) the page has two vertical rulings (see example) creating both the left and right margins. That assures all copy will be written within the range of the TelePrompTer lens field. Other newsrooms use similar rulings.

1.3   *Carbon Copies*

Most newsrooms will want multiple copies of news stories. Sometimes carbon paper is used, but often "books" of carbonless, color-coded paper are provided. There may be six or more pages in the book to be distributed to the variety of people who need them. Those people would include the producer, director, audio operator, TelePrompTer operator, graphics operator, and floor director, among others, including the anchor, of course. The presence of the TelePrompTer does not offer enough comfort for the anchor to dare go on the air without a script in hand. In radio a single carbon for file purposes may be all that is needed.

Typing Conventions

1.4   *The "Slug," Writer's Name, and Date*

Before beginning to write a story, identify it. In most newsrooms a story is given a "slug" when it is assigned to a reporter and will carry that same identifying label through the entire news process from assignment to the final air script. The story slug is usually determined by the assignment editor. As you begin to write the story, type in the one- or two-word slug in ALL CAPS in the upper left corner of the page. Immediately below that type in your name (just the last name will usually do) and below that, the date (just the day and month).

Some editors prefer to have the slug, name, and date typed as a single line across the top of the page, but that leaves little room for tape information, which we'll get to shortly. Yet others say to put it in the upper RIGHT corner. It depends on your newsroom's preference. For now, we'll use the upper left.

Now, space down about two inches before you start to write. This is very important because that room is needed for written instructions that may be added later.

1.5 *Using Standard Upper- and Lowercase*

Write in Standard upper- and lowercase. Some newsrooms prefer all uppercase while still others use special typewriters with larger-than-normal type faces. Most, however, use normal capitalization. The copy is easier to read, prevents confusion between common words and names (Green, for example), and signals the newsreader that a name is coming up so he or she won't get caught in an inflection trap.

1.6 *Triple Space*

Set your typewriter for TRIPLE space. All broadcast copy is triple-spaced to leave room for written corrections between the lines.

1.7 *Use Capital Letters Freely*

Certain key words and titles, which ordinarily might not be capitalized, can be in broadcast copy. The word Federal, for example, ordinarily is used lowercase unless in a formal title, but I have found it helps to capitalize it. In fact, capitalize freely to help the newsreader smooth out delivery. That's just a matter of personal preference. Some readers might object to the practice.

1.8   *One Story on a Page*

A couple of other simple-minded things: type only on one side of the paper and put only one story on a page, no matter how short it is or how closely it might be related to another story. That allows rearrangement of copy if needed. The exception would be when writing briefs or headlines that you know will air in the order in which you have written them.

Now that you have copy paper in the typewriter and have set the machine on triple space, and have written your slug and other information, and have left a two-inch margin at the top of the page, you are ready to begin writing. Push your tab key to indent five spaces and go to it.

1.9   *End Marks*

When you have written your story be sure to put some sort of end mark on it. That's where your center-of-page tab stop will be used. You will find different writers using distinctive end marks. The most common are -30-, -0-, XXXX or END. You should pick one and stick with it.

1.10   *Going to Page Two*

If your story is long and continues on a second page, type at the bottom of page one ((MORE)) and, with a copy pencil, draw a heavy arrow pointing to the right across the bottom of the page (you'll see how this is done in the examples). Note that the word ((MORE)) is in caps enclosed in double parentheses. That gives the news-reader an instant clue that the word is not to be read on the air, and that the story goes to page two.

1.11   *End every page with a complete sentence*

Always end page one with a COMPLETE sentence. NEVER break a sentence when going to page two. What if page two gets lost? Or if time is running low and you decide to drop page two? Disaster!

At the top of page two type the same slug word or phrase used to identify page one. It is not necessary to write in your name or the date on page two. Just the slug and a string of four 2222s. As in: INTERSTATE CRASH

2222. The same form is used for page 3333 and so on.
There is one school of thought that says to call page
two ADD ONE. I have always found that to be confusing
and do not recommend it. It's a holdover from newspaper
copy formats where it may have been useful in the
scissors-and-paste days.

Don't go to page two just for one or two more lines. Try
to leave about a one-inch margin at the bottom of the
page, but go ahead and put in an extra line if that's all you
have.

Timing

1.12 *Timing or line count*

When the story is complete, pencil in the approximate time or line count, depending on how it's done in
your newsroom, at the top right of page one. If the story
contains a tape insert, the running time of the tape should
also be written in.

Examples of Radio and TV Scripts

Other than the differing margin and tab setting, all of the
above applies to both radio and television scripting. Study the
examples of "typical" radio and TV script formats and see how
they differ.

Now, the differences between radio and television news
script writing become more dramatic.

Cuing Tapes for Radio and Television

1.13 *Writing a Tape Cue for Radio*

Cuing a tape for a radio newscast is a reasonably
simple procedure. Simply note at the top of the page that
a tape goes with the story and at the point where the tape
is to be used move the typewriter carriage to the right to
tab stop 10 (there it is, I told you we'd get to this), and
type in the "roll cue" in ALL CAPS. The sample copy
following illustrates this. A roll cue consists of the phrase

```
SLUG                  TAPE TIMING
NAME
DATE
10          20   25        50        80

((THIS GIVES THREE SECONDS A
LINE—TEN LINES = 30 SECONDS))

AUDIO CUES GO    ALL COPY GOES IN
IN THIS COLUMN   THIS COLUMN
```

ALL BROADCAST COPY IS <u>TRIPLE</u>

<u>SPACED</u>. <u>NEVER</u> WRITE TO THE END OF

A PAGE--LEAVE AT LEAST A ONE-INCH

MARGIN--GO TO NEXT PAGE WITH

((MORE)). <u>NEVER</u> BREAK A SENTENCE

AT THE END OF A PAGE. <u>ALWAYS</u> USE

SOME SORT OF END MARK. -0-, -30-,

XXXX, -END-.

-END-

Box 1.1
Typical Radio Script Format

BURGLAR
MACD
9/13

A 30-year-old Smallville man has been arrested in connection with a series of household break-ins.

Gaylord Swann of the 25-hundred block of Pelham Place was arrested late this morning on a warrant issued by Judge Charles Guernsey.

The warrant charges Swann with seven counts of breaking and entering over a period of four weeks.

In the past month, at least eleven local homes have been burglarized. Police estimate the total value of stolen goods to be in excess of 25-thousand dollars.

A preliminary hearing for Swann has been set for tomorrow at 2 P-M.

-0-

Box 1.2
Sample Radio Script

```
SLUG                    VIDEO TYPE AND TIME
NAME
DATE
     10         40    45 60        80

                        THIS GIVES TWO
                        SECONDS A LINE—
                        TEN LINES
                        = 20 SECONDS
ALL VIDEO AND           ALL COPY GOES IN
AUDIO                   THIS COLUMN

DIRECTIONS GO IN
THIS COLUMN
```

Box 1.3
Typical Television Script Format

```
VIDEO SIDE              |     SCRIPT SIDE
                        |
                        |
                        |
                        |
                        |
                        |
                        |
                        |
                        |     LIMIT OF WRITTEN
                        |     MATERIAL BEFORE
                        |     PAGE TWO
```

Box 1.4
Page Design Used by CNN and Others

```
BURGLAR                    TAPE :15
MACD
9/13

                    A 30-year-old Smallville
        man has been arrested in
        connection with a series of
        household break-ins.
                    Gaylord Swann of 25-38
        Pelham Place was arrested late
        this morning on a warrant issued
        by Judge Charles Guernsey.
                    Police Chief Sensor
        Calderara outlined the charges
        contained in the warrant.
    TAPE ON HERE.........RUNS :15...
        "THE LOUSY CREEP."
                    Calderara said there
        have been eleven burglaries in
        the last four weeks--the total
        value of stolen property is
        estimated to be more than 25-
        thousand dollars.
                    A preliminary hearing
        for Swann is set for tomorrow
        afternoon.
                        -0-
```

Box 1.5
Radio Script with Tape

TAPE ROLLS HERE, the timing of the tape and the last three or four words it contains. And that's about it for radio. A sample radio script with cues is shown in Box 1.5.

1.14 *Writing a Tape Cue for Television*

Television tape cuing presents a somewhat more complicated problem, largely because there are so many more people involved and all must know what is to happen. Furthermore, the medium is so much more complex that a lot of additional information has to be available to the production team.

Audio and Visual Effects

1.15 *Visual Effects*

For television, of course, we must deal with both audio and video cues and with a variety of visual enhancements such as superimpositions (supers), squeeze zooms, slides, chroma keys and so on. All these, if you want to use them, must be indicated on the script exactly the way they are to appear on the screen and at the precise moment needed. Often, however, it is not the writer, but the producer, who decides on video effects.

At the top of page one indicate that a tape goes with the story and give its timing and whether it is a voice-over (VO), which will probably be a silent (SIL) tape; that is, one with no sound track or with background sound only. If there is a voice track on the tape, that is called sound-on-tape (SOT).

1.16 *"Man On Camera."*

To begin, space down two inches and at tab stop 10 write MOC followed by a string of dots. That indicates "Man On Camera," and tells the director that the anchor's face should be on screen. Recently, as more and more anchors are female, "Man on Camera" is regarded as sexist. It has been suggested that MOC now means "Mike On Camera" in reference to the microphone. In any case, it still means the anchor's face (and mike, I suppose) is to be shown on the TV screen.

```
BURGLAR              VTR--SIL :30
MACD
9/13


MOC.........................A 30-year-

   old Smallville man has been

   arrested in connection with a

   series of household break-ins.

VTR ON HERE.............VO............:30

      Gaylord Swann of 25-38

   Pelham Place was arrested this

   morning on a warrant issued by

   Judge Charles Guernsey. Swann

   was taken into custody at his

   home by Police Chief Sensor

   Calderara and several other

   officers. Swann offered no

   resistance.
                ((MORE))
```

```
BURGLAR  2222        A police spokesman said

                    the warrant charges Swann with

                    seven counts of burglary over the

                    past four weeks. In all, there

                    have been eleven household

                    break-ins during that period.

                        Total property loss is

                    estimated at more than 25-

                    thousand dollars.

MOC  .........       A preliminary hearing

                    for Swann is set for tomorrow at

                    2 P-M.


                        -O-
```

Box 1.6
Sample Television Script with Silent (SIL) Tape

```
    BURGLAR              VTR--SOT :54
    MACD
    9/13


    MOC........................A 30-year-

        old Smallville man was arrested

        this morning in connection with a

        series of household break-ins.
    VTR ON HERE.............VO...........:09

            Police Chief Sensor

        Calderara and several other

        officers arrested Gaylord Swann

        at his Pelham Place home. Chief

        Calderara told a news conference

        about the charges.



    SOUND UP HERE.......RUNS :45......."THE

    LOUSY CREEP"

    ((SUPER: CHIEF S. CALDERARA))
                            ((MORE))
```

```
              BURGLAR 2222

MOC.........................A

        preliminary hearing for Swann is

        set for 2 P-M tomorrow.

                    -0-
```

Box 1.7
Sample Television Script with Sound-on-Tape (SOT)
and Super

1.17 *Tape Without Sound*

The anchor then reads the lead to the story and introduces the tape. At that point, you write (beginning at tab stop ten again) TAPE ROLLS HERE...VO...and the anchor continues to read as the picture shows what is on the tape, as illustrated here.

1.18 *Tape with Sound*

If there is a voice track on the tape, an interview, for example, that is to be cued after the anchor has read his or her portion, you write (at tab stop 10): SOUND UP HERE ...RUNS: 45..."THE LOUSY CREEP." That tells the director to have the audio controller bring up the sound track for 45 seconds until the "Out Cue" is heard, at which point he or she will "kill" the sound.

If at the end of the tape you wish to go back to the anchor's face, you once again write MOC...beginning in the far left margin at tab stop ten. I'm sure you've got the tab ten idea by now, so I won't say it again. A sample television script with sound-on-tape (SOT) and Superimposition is shown in Box 1.7.

1.19 *The Super and Other Effects*

There are so many gimmicks available to enhance a video story it is almost impossible to list them all and new ones appear frequently. Probably the most commonly used is the *super*. With an interview you will almost always want to super the subject's name. That needs to be spelled out in that wide left margin. Sometimes you will want to "key" in a piece of tape or a slide behind the anchor. That needs to go there, too. Just remember, EVERYTHING you want on the screen must be described in exact detail on the margin of the script, or it won't show up—at least not where or in the form you want it.

One of the great horrors of working in television is the number of hands that are in the soup. Each one is capable of the grossest error. As a writer, you are the first in a long line of people in a position to damage a perfectly good story. If you do your job well, it will lessen the chances of someone down the line botching his or hers.

PART II

GETTING WORDS ON PAPER

Forming Paragraphs
Indenting for paragraphs 2.1
Avoid hyphenating words between lines 2.2
Avoid hyphenating groups between lines 2.3
Clear and concise sentences 2.4

Simplifying numbers
Importance of Simplification 2.5
Rounding 2.6
Analogy 2.7
Approximation 2.8

Conventions of number usage
Areas of disagreement 2.9
Spell out one through eleven 2.10
Use numerals 12 through 999 2.11
Exceptions 2.12
Hyphenating number groups 2.13
Alphanumeric groups for large numbers 2.14
Avoid use of "point" in decimals 2.15
Express decimals as fractions 2.16
Age comes before name in identifiers 2.17
Street addresses expressed as numerals 2.18
Years usually written normally 2.19
Road and highway designations 2.20
Phone numbers and auto licenses 2.21

133,168

Pronunciation

The weather

Many new writers find getting started somewhat intimidating. It's really not hard. We'll try to lead you through the preliminary steps. There are lots of "rules" that you may find confusing at first. Don't worry too much about them—eventually, they'll come naturally.

Forming Paragraphs

2.1 *Indenting for paragraphs*

Indent normally for paragraphing. Again, some newsrooms prefer not to indent, but leave an extra blank line between paragraphs. That's probably all right, but the practice uses up a lot of paper. For our purposes, we'll indent. Indenting probably helps the reader.

2.2 *Avoid Hyphenating Words Between Lines*

There are some things done in normal writing that are never done in broadcast newswriting. NEVER, for example, hyphenate a word at the end of a line. If you are running out of room, strike out the word and start on the next line.

2.3 *Avoid Hyphenating Groups Between Lines*

You will find, however, a lot of hyphens are used in broadcast writing—in forming number groups and com-

bination phrases, for example. NEVER break a hyphenated group between lines.

2.4   Clear and Concise Sentences

Remember, we are not interested in how the copy
looks, here we are interested in making it easy to read and
easy to understand. One thing that helps is keeping
paragraphs short so each one contains one clear and
concise thought. Many broadcast writers will suggest
making each sentence a paragraph all by itself. That
certainly would make the editing process simpler and
probably help reading as well.

Simplifying Numbers

2.5   Importance of Simplification

If there is a key word in broadcast newswriting it is
simplify. Make things as easy to understand as you can
without getting simpleminded. Not everything, of course,
can handily be made simpler. Don't strain to do it, you'll
just sound silly.

Simplification is particularly important with large
numbers, which have a way of piling up in the ear and
never reaching the brain. If you can express a number in
such a way as to make it easier to understand you have
gone a long way toward the goal of helping your listeners.

Sometimes an exact number is necessary. In which
case, use it. Most often, however, you can simplify
numbers for the audience in one of several ways.

2.6   Rounding

Rounding: 1,348,975 is "more than one-and-one-
third million." See how easy it is?

2.7   Analogy (Comparison)

The analogy we use so much that it's now a cliché is
comparing the length of something to that of a football
field, where the playing area is 100 yards or 300 feet long.
With analogy, however, be careful that the object used for
comparison is fully familiar to the audience. Aunt Tillie

may not have the faintest idea what a football field even looks like, much less how long it is. Remember, too, that only the playing area is 300 feet—that doesn't count the end zones or stadium seats beyond.

2.8 *Approximation*

Approximate when necessary. For example, Albany is close to 150 miles from New York City. Actually, it's 156, but 150 is close enough for most uses.

Conventions of Number Usage

2.9 *Areas of Disagreement*

There are certain conventions for the use of numbers in broadcast news copy that make them easier to read and understand. Again, there are some areas of disagreement among professionals on details of number usage, but most are matters of personal style and not of great substance. What is presented here will generally be accepted as competent usage.

2.10 *Spell Out One through Eleven*

We prefer, for example, to spell out numbers one through eleven and one-hundred-eleven. Ordinal numbers are spelled out through eleventh, as in: first, fourth, etc. For higher numbers use 12th, 32nd 51st.

2.11 *Use Numerals 12 through 999*

All other numbers are expressed as figures up to 999. Some writers suggest writing out only single-digit numbers—that is, one through nine. Getting rid of the troublesome 11 and 111 is worth the additional effort.

2.12 *Exceptions*

As with so many rules there are exceptions to the above. When using numbers in compounds such as ages, always use the numeral: 6-year-old child. The same is true of street addresses and time: 5 o-clock, 3-57 14th Street; but it is five 13th Avenue. Another problem occurs when a number begins a paragraph. In that case, the number should be spelled out, even if it is usually written as a numeral. For example "Thirty-year-old Sam Smith has been arrested..." but, "A 30-year-old Smallville man..."

2.13 *Hyphenating Number Groups*

Please notice the hyphenations in the preceding paragraph. Hyphens play a heavy role in broadcast newswriting style. They are used to link the several connected parts of compounds such as two-million-dollars, four-and-a-half-percent, 15-cents. Because these are compounds (that is, the linked group of words and numbers expresses a single idea) they should NEVER be broken at the end of a line, just as a word is never hyphenated between lines.

2.14 *Alphanumeric Groups for Large Numbers*

Notice, too, that as we get into larger numbers—those above 999—we move into what our computer friends would call "the alphanumeric mode." This is the use of a combination of words and numerals to express numbers the same way we speak. It is considered poor style, although entirely correct in newswriting, to write two million-500-thousand or two-point-five-million. Instead, use two-and-a-half-million. It's more conversational and much easier to read and understand.

2.15 *Avoid Use of Point in Decimals*

Avoid using the word *point* where possible in dealing with decimals, especially when the decimal is less than one. A phrase like "point-seven-percent" is irritating. Such expressions are ugly and remote from conversational speech. Write "seven-tenths of one-percent" or, if the number is not really critical, "more than two-thirds." Note the use "...of one percent" not "...of a percent" which can be mistaken for eight percent.

2.16 *Express Decimals as Fractions*

Where possible, express decimals as fractions. So 0.75 becomes three-fourths (not three-quarters, by the way), 0.48 becomes nearly half and 0.55 is slightly more than half. Don't strain to make that change. It's better to sound natural than to reach too far for the conversion. Certain things, such as stock market reports, are often expressed as decimals and should be because that's the way listeners are accustomed to hearing them and the precise numbers are very important to some people.

2.17 *Age Comes Before Name in Identifiers*

Ages will normally come before the name in a combined identifier: "23-year-old Sue Jones." However, to vary things write "Sue Jones, who is 23," or where the age is important, "Sue Jones received her first book contract at the age of 23."

2.18 *Street Addresses Expressed as Numerals*

Street addresses should always be expressed as numerals except when the number is a single digit: 5–23 Walnut Avenue; five Courtland Center; 43–27 Holmes Street.

2.19 *Years usually Written Normally*

Years should be as normal: 1985. Some writers prefer 19–85. That's okay if your newsreader doesn't object. I personally find it jarring.

2.20 *Road and Highway Designations*

Become familiar with the conventions of road and highway designations in the area and the local idiom used to refer to them. "Rural route" for example, doesn't mean the same thing everywhere. In copy one would write I-81, U-S route 2–20, state route 6–46, or Virginia 6–46, (it's ROOT, by the way, not ROUT) according to local custom.

2.21 *Phone Numbers and Auto Licenses*

We are rarely, but occasionally, called upon to put such things as phone numbers or auto license numbers in our copy. Here each numeral is to be pronounced as a word, so hyphenate and write: "That number is 4-6-3-7-0-

3-6," or if local custom permits: "4-6-3-70-36." "The license number is Virginia V-A-V-3-0-5." Some writers would express the number as "V-A-V-3-OH-5." Whatever you feel most comfortable with is best. The point here is that the hyphens tell the newscaster that each unit of the number is to be pronounced as an individual word. When giving a phone number it's a good idea to warn your listeners they may want to jot something down and then repeat the number at least once.

Names

2.22 *How to Simplify*

As with numbers, try to simplify names as well. You might wonder how that can be done. In many instances there's not much you can do, but there are also numerous cases where certain elements of individual names are not needed.

2.23 *Avoid Full Names of the Very Prominent*

It's not necessary to use the full same of the President of the United States or the governor of the state where you're working. Often, there will be persons locally who are well-enough known to be referred to only by title and last name.

2.24 *Avoid Junior, Senior, Third, etc.*

Drop Junior, Senior, Third, etc, unless there is a real possibility of confusing the subject of the story with a relative of the same name. Often the newswriter has no way of knowing and neither does the audience. However, there are exceptions to this rule: Sammy Davis Junior is not simply Davis—the Junior is needed because it has become part of his full name through repeated use. There are other similar cases.

2.25 *Avoid Middle Names and Initials*

We normally dispense with middle names or initials. Again, exceptions loom large. No one would recognize Robert Lee as being anyone special until he is referred to as Robert E. Lee. John Foster Dulles was not simply John Dulles. When a person's name is especially well-known, follow the common use of that name. Jerry Lewis and Jerry Lee Lewis are two very different persons. However, lesser-known individual's names lend themselves to simplification. This is especially true in police and court cases where the individual involved is almost always referred to in official documents by all the names he may have: e.g., Billy Rayjoe Huntsbarger. In most cases you will be on safe ground just calling him Billy Huntsbarger along with the other usual identification.

2.26 *Don't Use Both Full- and Nickname*

There's one other way a name can be simplified—or at least shortened. In cases where a person is known by both a formal first name and a nickname: e.g., Congressman Thomas P. "Tip" O'Neill. In broadcast news copy refer to him as either Thomas or Tip, but not both. Pick one and stick with it.

2.27 *Second References*

Normally, the subject of the story or quoted source is referred to by first and last name and title, if any, on first reference, then by last name only in subsequent references. In the case of women this becomes somewhat awkward. Note that an unknown woman, Mrs. Blanche Smith, will be referred to on second and subsequent references as Smith. However, women of stature, such as British Prime Minister Margaret Thatcher, will almost always be referred to by title or as Mrs. in later references. It's considered a mark of respect for the title, but it does create an inconsistency.

2.28 *Use of Abbreviated Titles*

All titles are spelled out fully except Mr., Mrs., and Ms. We use Mr. because it cannot be confused with anything else; we use Mrs. because it is an abbreviation of mistress and you certainly would not want to use that, and we use Ms (no period, note) because it stands for nothing and cannot be spelled out. Some writers say Dr. is permissible. I disagree after having met Doctor Drive, whose name could be abbreviated as Dr. Dr. That's rough on copy readers.

All titles except Mr., Mrs. and Ms are to be spelled out. That includes Professor, Doctor, Lieutenant Colonel, Private First Class and Reverend.

2.29 *The Clergy*

And that brings us to the clergy. We will not attempt here to get into the complexities of forms of address and titles of the various denominations. Both the AP and UPI Style Books have excellent discussions of the form for clerical titles. If in doubt, call the man or woman in question and ask. Remember, forms of address vary widely from one denomination to another and it is possible to offend deeply by using the wrong form of title or address. Another thing to remember: Reverend is an honorific denoting a member of the clergy, not part of the person's name, so the reference is always to "The Reverend."

Acronyms and Abbreviations

2.30 *The Acronym*

We live in a world of acronyms—a word made up of the first letters of each word in a long title, such as "NATO." Acronyms are fine in broadcast copy as long as they are well-known to the public at large. Deciding that is usually a matter of your own familiarity with the name. NATO certainly is okay to use on first reference, so is "RADAR." The audience would be less well-informed if you used North Atlantic Treaty Organization or RAdio Detecting And Ranging device. To be a true acronym the formation must be a pronounceable word.

2.31 *Other Initial Abbreviations*

There are many groups of initials we frequently use that cannot be pronounced but are preferred over the full name of the organization: N-double-A-C-P, is an example. However, AFL-CIO is considered an exception to the hyphenation rule because it is difficult to write when it is written as A-F-L-C-I-O.

2.32 *Use of Hyphens and Periods in Abbreviations*

Note the hyphenation when each letter is to be pronounced as a separate word and the lack of hyphens in the true acronyms, where the whole group of letters is pronounced as one word. Note too, we use hyphens where in normal writing there would be periods. Another rule exception: only in the case of a person's initials do we use periods, otherwise use hyphens. It is H.L. Mencken, but U-S, U-N and P-M.

2.33 *The abbreviation of State, City and Street Names*

We've already discussed the nonabbreviation of most titles. The same rule applies to just about everything else that you want pronounced fully. Do not abbreviate the words Street, Place, Drive, and so on. Do not abbreviate the names of the states. Do not abbreviate directions such as West or North. Intermediate compass points are written as one word: Northwest, but East Southeast. Do not abbreviate the names of cities such as Saint Louis. I must admit some writers claim St. is all right because it is so well-known. But, it can be confused with street and, as Murphy assures us, if something can be confused it will be.

2.34 *The Use of A.M. and P.M.*

Some writers, in an effort to be more conversational, advise us to avoid the use of a.m. and p.m. and instead say "this morning" or "tomorrow afternoon." I really don't object to A-M and P-M, but they must be written in CAPS and with a hyphen.

Contractions

2.35 *The Use of Contractions*

There are differing schools of thought on the use of contractions. Some writers believe the use of contractions makes the copy less formal and more conversational. That may be true, but it can also lead to misunderstanding. That is especially true of negative contractions where the "n't" can easily be missed by either the reader or the listener. *Can't* can be confused with *can—cannot*

cannot. Often, too, you will want to use the "not" for emphasis. There is no problem with the use of some contractions such as that's, there's, there'll and so on. Won't is probably the only negative contraction that's safe. It cannot be confused with its complete form, will not. But, there are parts of the country where "want" sounds just like "won't."

Plurals and Possessives

2.36 *Collective Nouns*

Collective nouns give many writers special problems. Again, it probably has to do with the emphasis on colloquial and conversational style rather than on literary correctness. There is the argument that certain constructions, although grammatically correct, sound horrid when spoken. An example is the treatment of the word *couple* as a collective noun. In some instances it must be a collective, but in others it is strained, at best. "The couple are going," is clearly wrong. However, listen to this: "The couple is going; it will arrive in an hour." That's awful. "The couple is going," is fine and correct. But to refer to the couple as "it," in the second part of that sentence, although correct and agreeing with the first phrase, is grating on the ear and so far from colloquial speech as to make the meaning unclear. If the collective noun in that example were *family* or *team*, however, it would be treated as a singular. Write what sounds best and poses the least threat to the sentence.

Other collective nouns that should be treated as singulars unless the meaning of the sentence is endangered are such words as dollars (when referring to a bulk of money), miles, council, team and committee.

2.37 *Singulars That Look Like Plurals*

The special problems brought up by collective singulars that look like plurals cause real trouble. One-million dollars has been spent. Here, dollars looks plural, but it's really singular because what we are talking about is a single unit of one million dollars, not one million individual dollars. The same reasoning holds true for the other examples above and many others.

2.38 *Proper Names Ending in "S"*

Also troublesome for broadcasters are proper names that end with *s*. Dealing with plurals and possessives of such names can be maddening. Let's use Jones as an example. The plural of Jones is Joneses. The singular possessive can be either Jones' or Jones's, both pronounced Joneses. The plural possessive is Joneses'. Got that?

Also when dealing with names that end in *s* keep in mind how they will sound on the air. "Hodges's body" sounds terrible—rewrite. "The victim's body..." sounds much better. The name and body don't have to go side-by-side.

Listener Problems

2.39 *Avoid Writing What the Audience Must Figure Out*

Never write anything the listener has to figure out. He or she doesn't have time. Remember, the listener has no way of knowing where your sentence is going until he or she hears it all.

If the listener has to stop listening part way through to figure out some math problem or decide what you mean by "two days later," he or she will lose the sense of what you're trying so hard to say.

2.40 *Small Math Problems*

Always do the math. Often stories will appear with a lead like "Six men have been named to the Island Pond Chamber of Commerce Committee on Roach Control." Then in the body of the story, seven men are named. This is so common a fault, as is the inborn inability of reporters to add columns of figures, that every time numbers appear in a story they should be checked. Take no one's calculations for granted. Always do the math.

Punctuation

2.41 *The Importance of Punctuation*

Proper punctuation is just as important in broadcast news copy as in any other form of writing. It is necessary for the writer to learn its somewhat different form, and to recognize that news anchors frequently have personal preferences on sentence structure.

Punctuation in broadcast news copy is somewhat modified from normal usage to help the person who has to read the copy on the air.

2.42 *Use of Dashes*

Use periods normally at the end of sentences. However, use many dashes rather than commas and semicolons. Set off phrases--such as this one--with dashes. A dash on a standard typewriter is formed by using a double hyphen--like that. Dashes tell the news-reader that a pause longer than a comma calls for is needed, and inflection may need to be altered. Dashes also can be used where a comma normally would be placed to help the story flow.

Use commas normally in separating words in a series and to separate the names of cities and states as in Helena, Montana.

2.43 *Avoid Parentheses*

NEVER use parentheses. Parentheses are used only to set off material in the body of the story that is not intended to be read on the air—((PAUSE))—for example. Note the parentheses are doubled and the instruction to the reader is written in all CAPS to further assure it will not be read aloud. If you must use a parenthetical phrase —and usually you should not—set it off with dashes. If you find you have written a sentence that needs a paren-thetical phrase to explain it, you have written a bad sentence for broadcast news use and you should start over. Remember: simplify. Keep your sentences short, clean, direct and uncomplicated.

2.44 *Avoid Quotations*

Do not use quotation marks. In fact, avoid using direct quotations wherever possible. There are times, of course, when a person's exact words are necessary. In those cases, use the exact words, but precede them with some sort of introductory phrase such as "These were his exact words," or something similar. If the quotation is long, it's a good idea to interject a phrase such as: "still quoting" somewhere midway. Do not EVER say "quote" and "unquote." That is a hold over from the ancient days of sending news by telegraph when the sending operator wanted to be certain the receiving end knew the limits of the quoted material. And, for Heaven's sake, don't write the inanity: "He said in his words," he can't say it in anyone else's.

2.45 *Avoid First-Person Quotations*

NEVER use a personal quotation—that is, a quotation including personal pronouns or references such as "I," "We," and "You." That confuses the listener as to who is saying it—the newsreader or the person quoted. Paraphrase all personal quotations except where the exact words are needed to avoid confusion or when they are so outrageous that's the only safe way to put them on the air.

2.46 *Symbols*

Most other punctuation is to be avoided in broadcast copy. ! @ # $ % & * − + = have no place in what we're doing. They cannot be pronounced.

Editing

2.47 *Errors in Copy*

Even though you may be a whiz on the typewriter, you're bound to make mistakes. There are ways to correct them—but the anchor isn't going to tolerate messy copy. "Dirty" copy is considered a sign of an unreliable writer. There's no time in broadcasting to do much rewriting, so the trick is to make the copy as clean as possible the first time through. The advent of computer terminals in broadcast newsrooms will make editing almost painless —but will also leave no excuse for copy errors. Not all errors are as simple as typos, of course—mistakes in facts or omissions are not easily forgiven.

2.48 *Keep Editing Simple*

Copy editing for broadcast news is relatively simple beside the complexities of print media editing. There is one basic idea to keep in mind: some poor soul—you or someone else—is going to have to read this mess aloud before an audience. Therefore, you keep your editing as clean and simple as possible.

2.49 *Avoid Proofreader's Marks*

Never use newspaper editing marks. They mean nothing to a broadcaster and just mess up the copy.

2.50 *Correcting an Error*

If you have made an error—a typo or the wrong word or whatever—COMPLETELY OBLITERATE the offending word and write the correction in block printing above the error. NEVER change just one or two letters in a word —change the whole word. If you catch the error while the story is still in your typewriter, of course, you can X-out the bad word and type the correction in above it.

2.51 *Exceptions*

If you fail to indent for a paragraph, forget it—don't use a proofreader's graph mark. If you type a lowercase letter where you want a capital, go ahead and block print the capital over the little letter (these rules are not carved in stone), so long as it is clearly legible.

2.52 *Inserting Omitted Material*

If you have left out some material that needs to be inserted into the body of a story, print it in between the lines if its only a few words. If it's going to take more than one line, retype the whole story.

Pronunciation

2.53 *Pronouncers*

You may not have seen this word before. It is the word commonly used to describe phonetically-written pronunciation guides in broadcast copy. The guides are usually ad hoc—that is, made up by the writer as he or she goes along—but they do emerge remarkably alike from various writers.

2.54 *Use of Guides*

Every newsroom should have a pronunciation guide to unusual (or unusually pronounced) local family and place names. USE THE GUIDE.

2.55 *Effects of Mispronunciations*

There is nothing that will kill the reputation and credibility of a news operation more quickly and more thoroughly than the mispronunciation of well-known local names. How can the audience depend on the accuracy of the facts of your story if you don't even know basic things like the pronunciation of local names? Correct pronunciation—that is, "correct" in your locality —is crucially important. This cannot be stressed too strongly.

2.56 *Watch for Local Anomalies*

Near the locality where this is written, for example, there is a city named Buena Vista. Every person who knows anything about language recognizes that as a Spanish name, meaning roughly "pretty view." And, in Spanish it is pronounced BWAYN-uh VEES-tuh. But here it is pronounced BYOO-nuh VIHS-tuh.

2.57 *Writing Pronouncers in Copy*

Note how the pronunciation guide is written in the above paragraph. That is called *phonetic spelling* and that is the way all pronunciation guides should be written for broadcast—in such a way as to provide the actual sound of the word. This is the ONLY way to write pronouncers —as they are called—for broadcast news copy. Do not underline stressed syllables. Do not use dictionary-type diacritical marks. Do not—as the wire services do—use an apostrophe to indicate stress. (The wire service broadcast news circuits use all uppercase, so they cannot use upper- and lowercase to indicate stressed syllables).

Sometimes it is helpful to the reader to use the "rhymes-with" approach to pronunciation. Write "Wythe ((RHYMES WITH SMITH))." Note that in all cases, the pronouncer is enclosed in double parentheses following the troublesome word. Particularly when writing for someone else, use pronouncers freely. It is not necessary to write in a pronouncer more than once except in difficult cases. If the word or name is too difficult, it's probably better to work around it on subsequent references.

2.58 *Wire Service Pronunciation Guides*

The AP and UPI both have pronunciation guides in their style handbooks. In addition, they provide pronouncers for unusual names that come into the news on a day-to-day basis. When you are rewriting wire copy, however, you should convert their method of depicting pronunciation to the method we have discussed here, which is simply showing stressed syllables in uppercase and unstressed ones in lowercase and showing vowel sounds phonetically—the way they sound.

The Weather

2.59 *A Bad Spell of Weather*

What is it about the weather? We hear more barbarous use of language in television weather programs than in almost any other instance, except in the sports and that's a lost cause, I fear. The weather may be, too. Weathermen and women on television, apparently trying to be informal or cute, come up with some real whoppers. It seems as though they're not thinking about the logic of what they are saying.

2.60 *Mangled Language*

"Three inches of rainfall has fallen." "We can expect a 40-percent chance of rainfall tomorrow." No; a chance of rain, perhaps, but not rainfall. Rainfall is rain that has already fallen. We predict rain, we measure rainfall. "Rain shower activity," is another one. A shower is by definition both rain and an activity. That's a double-headed redundancy. When there is talk of snow "showers" what they really mean is snow flurries.

2.61 Some Examples

How often have you heard it said that the thermometer is falling? It'll break. It's the temperature that's falling, not the thermometer. What about "temperatures will warm up?" No. The weather will warm up, temperatures will rise. There is one accepted use in which a weather instrument is said to be moving. The old sea-dog who says "The glass is falling (or rising)" as he looks at his barometer. That's informal, at best.

How's this for mind-bending logic? "We can expect a widely scattered shower." How can one shower be scattered, even widely? Think about what you are saying—make sense.

A few other weather observations. In my opinion, Celsius is dead; has been since 1744. It confuses a lot of people to have to deal with two sets of temperature figures, one of which is generally meaningless. On the other hand, the United States is home to many people who have come from foreign lands where the metric system—including Celsius temperature measurement— is in use. There is disagreement among news people whether to use the Celsius reading or not. A lot may depend on where you are. In a major metropolitan area with significant foreign population, it's use might be advisable.

The word *presently* is not synonymous with *currently*. To say "the temperature is presently 60 degrees" is nonsense. Presently means "soon," "in the near future." Some authorities have caved in on this one and are saying presently means both now and soon. That, too, is nonsense.

The winds are calm. Think about it. If the air is calm, there is no wind, so winds cannot be calm. There may be no wind, in which case say there is no wind, or the air is calm.

Only when referring to wind do we use the compass point it is coming FROM. In all other references to direction we speak of the point toward which something is moving. A northerly wind blows a boat in a southerly direction.

2.62 *Chamber of Commerce Mentality*

Finally, on a somewhat different plane, serious thought needs to be given to what might be called the Chamber of Commerce approach to weather: sun is good, rain is bad, hot is bad, cold is bad, mild is good. Radio and TV weatherpeople speak of the "threat" or "risk" of rain or snow. Surely, there are few times when the words threat or risk are not overstating the case. This is not to say that weather warnings should be avoided—but let's save some words for when we really need them.

THE WIRE SERVICES

Virtually every newsroom will have at least one national wire circuit—either The Associated Press (AP) or United Press International (UPI). There are certain things you need to know about them.

State Bureaus

3.1   *The Bureaus*

Most states have at least one "bureau," often more than one. The bureaus are the collection and dissemination points for news in their states.

3.2   *Schedules*

Each main bureau—usually in the state's capital city —has a schedule it follows for sending out news of statewide interest. You should have a copy of that schedule posted in your newsroom so you will know what to expect and when. The state bureau feeds the wire circuit about 20 minutes out of each hour. The rest of the time the circuit is carrying the output of the national wire service and there is also a schedule of the routine news and features that come down the wire from national.

3.3   *Sharing with your wire service*

Both the AP and the UPI depend on member stations to share their news—called "protecting" them. That means that when you develop a local story that might have wider interest or appeal, you send it on to the state bureau—after you have used it yourself, of course. That also goes for any audio tapes that might accompany the story. Some newsrooms subscribe to both wire services, so it's up to the local news director to decide which he or she will "protect" on a given story.

3.4   *Advisories and Notes*

There are certain things that "move" on the wires that are not intended for broadcast—notes to editors, news directors or station managers—various advisories, schedules of audio feeds and the like. These should be saved and passed on to the people who need to see them.

Contents

3.5   *Warnings on Content*

Often a story will be preceded by a note. Sometimes the note will indicate that the story contains material some people might find objectionable. In that case read the story carefully to decide in rewriting whether the material is really all that bad. If it is, leave it out.

3.6   *Embargoes*

The note might indicate that the story is "embargoed" for broadcast before a stated time. Usually an embargo is imposed by the source. The Governor, for example, might not want the advance story on his or her speech to be broadcast prior to its delivery. Embargoes should be obeyed. No one is held in lower esteem by fellow journalists than the person who "breaks" an embargo. Once broken, however, the story is out and everyone is free to use it.

3.7   *KILLS*

Always obey any "KILL" notice. That indicates the story in question is either wrong or in serious doubt and must not be used. If it is used after a KILL advisory is sent on the wire, any subsequent action, such as a lawsuit, will be filed against the broadcaster who used the story.

Alert Levels

3.8   *Wire Service Alerts*

The wire services have established several levels of alerts which are signalled by a series of bells on the printer.

3.9   *Urgent*

Three bells indicates a story coming that is slugged "URGENT." It is the lowest level of alert and may be a story about a late-breaking development but not of overriding public importance.

3.10   *Bulletin*

The next level is "BULLETIN" which is preceded by five bells. A bulletin is usually the first news about a major story.

3.11   *Flash*

The final level is "FLASH." It is reserved for only the most shattering stories. It is preceded by ten bells and is usually very tersely worded: PRESIDENT SHOT. A flash is a very rare event.

PART IV

USAGE GUIDE

Introduction

There is no excuse for a professional writer to use the language in a sloppy or plainly incorrect manner.

Misuse of the language is malpractice.

Words are the tools of the journalist, whether working in print or broadcasting. As with any craft or art, the tools must be of the highest quality, kept in good condition, and used with care and precision.

There are disagreements among excellent writers on matters of usage but most would not condone careless misuse.

So many misuses and careless uses have crept into our daily speech it is not possible to catalogue them all. Those included here are frequently heard and constitute some of the worst of the linguistic pollution.

We are not talking about slang here—most slang has no place in newswriting. What we are about to examine are examples of the common misuse of ordinary words. Every writer has favorite linguistic horrors heard or seen with distressing frequency, and that's what leads us to compile usage guides.

This guide is intended to be especially for broadcast writers but one will find many entries that would apply to all good writing. All of these have been collected through listening and reading. Some are included because they are frequently mispronounced, not necessarily misused. Some of the entries would not be considered "good" words for broadcast news. Use words that are comfortable for you—that fit easily on your tongue. If you are uncomfortable, your audience will sense that discomfort and that will impede efficient communication.

Many words have many meanings. For the most part we will

look at the primary or most common meanings and usages. After all, we are trying to communicate—so we should do it in the least complicated and most readily understood way we can.

While getting all sounds on paper is difficult (the TH sound in *Smith* and *with* differ, for example), this phonetic guide will aid you in understanding the usage guide as well as help you create useful pronouncers. It is based on the guide used by the UPI.

VOWELS

A   Use AY for long A as in mate.

Use A for short A as in cat.

Use AI for nasal A as in air.

Use AH for short A as in father.

Use AW for broad A as in talk.

E   Use EE for long E as in meet.

Use EH for short E as in get.

Use UH for hollow E as in the or the French article le.

Use AY for the French long E with accent as in Pathé.

Use IH for E as in pretty.

Use EW for EW as in few.

I   Use EYE for long I as in time.

Use EE for French long I as in machine.

Use IH for short I as in pity.

O   Use OH for long O as in note.

Use AH for short O as in hot.

Use AW for broad O as in fought.

Use OO for O as in fool.

Use U for O as in foot.

Use OW for O as in how.

U   Use EW for long U as in mule.

Use OO for long U as in rule.

Use U for middle U as in put.

Use UH for short U as in shut.

CONSONANTS

Use K for hard C as in cat.
Use S for soft C as in cease.
Use SH for soft CH as in machine.
Use CH or TCH for hard CH as in catch.
Use Z for hard S as in disease.
Use S for soft S as in sun.
Use G for hard G as in gang.
Use J for soft G as in general.

The Usage Guide

A/An The rule of thumb (or tongue) here is if the first sound of the following word is a vowel use *AN*, if the sound is a consonant you want *A*. It's the sound that's important, not the spelling. I still cling to "an historic...," even though many experts now claim because the "H" in history is sounded the word should be preceded by *A*.

Ability/Capacity *ABILITY* is simply the power to do something. *CAPACITY* has to do with the power to hold or contain.

About/Almost/Around These words are frequently used interchangeably, but there is a distinction. *ABOUT* and *AROUND* are references to place, while *ALMOST* refers to number or quantity.

Above When used as a back reference, as in "as mentioned ABOVE," the word only sends the listener racing through his or her memory to try to recall what you're talking about—thereby missing the rest of the story. Avoid such use. The same can be said for such back references as *former* and *latter*.

Accelerate Pronounced ak-CELL-ur-ayt.

Accessory Pronounced ak-SESS-ur-ee. There is no such word as *assessory*. An *ACCESSORY* is a person indirectly involved in a crime: accessory before or after the fact. The word is also used to describe an article that may be enhancing, such as a necklace or whitewall tires.

Accident/Mishap Some news writers try to avoid the word ACCIDENT in highway crash stories, contending they are seldom truly accidents, but caused by carelessness or stupidity. That may be a bit extreme, but it does point up the real meaning of the word. An accident is an event that occurs without planning or direct cause. A MISHAP is a minor accident, so a serious auto crash should not be termed a mishap.

Accused/Alleged/Suspected ACCUSED carries the connotation of a formal charge. ALLEGED is an assertion of truth—or questionable truth—but does not indicate a charge has been made. SUSPECTED is about the same as accused. Alleged and suspected should be used with great care in crime stories. Make sure someone has made the allegation.

Acme/Epitome ACME is pronounced AK-mee, EPITOME is pronounced ee-PIT-uh-mee. Acme means the summit, the top, the best. Epitome means the best example, a typical representation, ideal form. There is another, uncommonly used meaning of epitome, which is to represent in brief or summary form.

Acre/Tract ACRE and TRACT both refer to land. It is redundant to write "An acre of land." You can't have an acre of anything else. Tract, however, does have other meanings—as in political or religious tracts—pamphlets, theses. However, when the context of the story clearly relates to land, tract standing alone is preferred.

Adapt/Adopt These are somewhat related words that are often confused. ADAPT means to adjust or to accommodate, to make suitable to the situation. Earlier it was pointed out that a newswriter must adapt to the style in use in the newsroom. ADOPT means to take on a change or relationship. In the above sentence, we could have said a newswriter must adopt the style of the newsroom.

Addict An ADDICT is a person physically habituated to a substance or some other addictive thing. It should not be used in the sense of having the practice of or being a devotee. A person may be devoted to classical music—but would not be called an addict.

Ade/Aid/Aide ADE is a kind of soft drink made with sweetened fruit juice and water—lemonade (note spelling). To AID is to give help or support. An *AIDE* is a person whose job is to provide help or support for a person of rank. Originally it was aide-de-camp, meaning an assistant to a military officer, now shortened to aide and broadened in meaning to refer to virtually anyone who is hired in a support or advisory position.

Adjacent/Contiguous   *ADJACENT* in most common use means to be nearby, but not touching. *CONTIGUOUS* means to be touching along boundaries. "Virginia and North Carolina are contiguous states." "The West Indies is a group of adjacent islands."

Admit/Confess   *ADMIT* has a number of meanings, probably the most common of which is to allow to enter. Another common use has to do with acknowledging fact—the witness admits to having seen the crime. However, it does not have the sense of *CONFESS*, in the acknowledgment of one's guilt, either in court or as a penitent before a priest, although it is frequently used that way. In your copy, use *confess* when you're talking about a criminal telling what he or she did. Not only is it more precise, it also avoids a possible confusion. In court, a judge is said to admit evidence when he or she allows it to be placed in the record.

Adopted/Adoptive   The child is *ADOPTED*, the parents and siblings are said to be *ADOPTIVE*.

Adverse/Averse   *ADVERSE* means opposing, acting against. *AVERSE* means to have a feeling of dislike or distaste.

Advice/Advise   *ADVICE* is the noun, *ADVISE* is the verb form. Advice is what an *advisor* gives.

Aerial/Antenna   There was a time when *ANTENNAS* were called *AERIALS*, but now the accepted term is antenna.

Affect/Effect   The confusion with this pair will probably be with us forever. *AFFECT* means to influence or to have a bearing upon someone or something. *EFFECT* means to bring about, to accomplish. That is the verb form. As a noun, you almost always want *effect*. "She was deeply affected by his presence." "That was the exact effect he wanted."

Affidavit   A document, usually legal, containing a statement made under oath. A deposition in which testimony is

sworn. Note especially the spelling—it is *affiDAVIT*, not
...david.

Affinity Except in some scientific applications such as particle
physics, only people feel an *AFFINITY* toward one
another. The word originally had to do with marriage, but
now means a general attraction. It does not mean a liking
for something other than another human. A person might
have a deep liking for reading, for example, but would not
be said to have an affinity for it. Again, we're up against
common usage, which is probably going to broaden the
definition.

Affluent/Effluent *AFFLUENT* is an adjective usually indicating
wealth—"our affluent society." It has the sense of a
strong flow. *EFFLUENT* also has the sense of flowing, but
usually refers to an environmental pollutant such as
sewage.

Aftermath *AFTERMATH* always follows something bad—such
as a flood or fire. It is the resulting devastation. It is not
correct to refer to the aftermath of an election or a party,
unless it was one stupendous party!

Afterward/Toward/Forward These and other words such as
anyway, anywhere, and so on, do not have a final "s."

Aggravate *AGGRAVATE* means to make worse in degree.
"His cold was aggravated by the wet weather." It does not
have a meaning of pester or tease, except in the most
informal use.

Alibi/Excuse An *ALIBI* is a specific rebuttal of evidence based on
place. That is, the accused person can prove he or she was
somewhere other than at the scene of the crime when the
crime was committed. It is not a general *EXCUSE* although
some dictionaries cite such usage.

All...Is Not... Be very careful of this construction. It will very
often say just exactly opposite of what you want. "All
that glitters is not gold." Think about it. That really says
that nothing that glitters is gold, which we know is not
true. (The Shakespeare quotation actually used the word
"glisters," but that is too odd) The construction has a
touch of class about it, but it can be very tricky. During
the 1984 Summer Olympics we were told "All the
marathon runners will not finish." Think about it.

Allergic The primary (and I would suggest only) meaning of *ALLERGIC* has to do with disease—to be allergic to some food or other substance that makes one ill. It is possible to say one is allergic to another person—offended or put off by him or her—but I would consider that to be non-standard. Webster's accepts it.

All Right/Alright *ALL RIGHT* means satisfactory, acceptable, suitable and so on. *ALRIGHT* means exactly the same thing but is considered nonstandard.

All Together/Altogether *ALL TOGETHER* and *ALTOGETHER* express altogether different ideas. *All together* means just that—we are all together, a group. *Altogether* means in the entirety: "there are 510 books, altogether."

Allude/Elude To *ALLUDE* to something is to make an indirect reference. To *ELUDE* is to evade cleverly. Both words come from the Latin *ludere*, which means to play.

Allusion/Illusion An *ALLUSION* is an indirect reference, a hint. An *ILLUSION* is a misleading image or idea—an optical illusion, for instance.

Almost/Most Do not use *MOST* in the sense of nearly, not quite. "Most all of us were there," is unacceptable, while "Most of us were there" is all right. Test each usage to see if *ALMOST* may be what you want.

A Lot This is a two-word phrase. A few years ago the "word" *alot* started showing up in student's work. It persists. The colloquial "quite a lot" or "I feel a lot better" are not acceptable as standard English, although the expressions are certainly widely used and readily understood to mean a great deal or considerably. They are imprecise and probably should not be used in broadcast news copy.

Altar/Alter An *ALTAR* is a raised platform on which religious rituals are performed. Originally it was a place of sacrifice. *ALTER* means to change.

Alter Ego Literally, "another I." Correctly used, *ALTER EGO* refers to someone very close with whom intimate things are shared—another self. It does not mean, except in psychological circles, a second personality or another phase of one's personality.

Alternate/Vacillate/Oscillate Many words in our language have a sense of number built-in. *ALTERNATE* is one of them.

It means first one, then the other—between two (and only two) points. You should not confuse it with *VACILLATE* which means to waiver, be uncertain; or with *OSCILLATE* which means to swing back and forth or up and down, like a pendulum or a sine wave.

Alternative   Knowing that *alternate* has the built-in sense of two, the number of choices we face when we have *ALTERNATIVES* cannot exceed two. It is possible to have more than two courses of action, but in that case you have choices, not alternatives. Admittedly, alternative is used in a casual way to mean two or more choices, but that's not strictly precise.

Alumna/Alumnae/Alumni/Alumnus   Girls and boys together. One does not have to be a graduate of a school to be considered an *alum(na)(nus)*, one merely has to have been enrolled at some point. *ALUMNA* is a feminine alum, *ALUMNAE* is the plural, but *alumna* is also accepted; an *ALUMNUS* is the male counterpart, and *ALUMNI* is the masculine plural. Alumni is also used to refer to all who have attended a coeducational institution.

Amateur   An *AMATEUR* is one who pursues a hobby, sport, or other activity just for the fun of it. An amateur is not necessarily clumsy or new to the activity. Therefore, to refer to someone who is inept as acting in an "amateurish fashion" is not necessarily correct. Words you may want are *neophyte, novice,* or *tyro,* all of which mean new to the activity or inexperienced, unskilled.

Ambivalence/Indecision   Like *alternative, AMBIVALENCE* suggests two and only two positions or attitudes: love-hate, for example. The two sides are very often seen as being in conflict. It goes beyond mere *INDECISION,* which is a broader term.

America/Canada   *AMERICA* usually refers to the United States. However, in a story in which both the United States and *CANADA* are mentioned, it is best to recognize that Canada, in fact, is also part of North America and make your reference to "Canada and the United States," and not to "Canada and America." The same can be said for any nation of the Americas—North, Central, or South.

America's Cup   The sailing trophy awarded following an elimination race between two vessels approximately every four years is named for the yacht *America* which won the first cup in competition off the English coast in 1851. It is always written as a possessive—with an apostrophe. There is also the Americas Cup, in golf, without the apostrophe. Confusing? Certainly!

Amok/Amuck   The correct spelling is *AMOK* and refers to an uncontrollable frenzy. The term originated in Malaysia, but has now entered English with exactly the same meaning. *AMUCK* is a common English spelling, but is considered nonstandard.

Among/Between   Do we even need to discuss this after all these years? I think so, because the misuse continues. Use *AMONG* when three or more persons or things are involved. Use *BETWEEN* when there are only two. A team does not share its prize *between* its members, unless there are only two.

Amoral/Immoral   *AMORAL* means nonmoral, neither moral nor immoral. *IMMORAL* means not moral, inconsistent with good behavior.

Amphitheater   Look at the word. It is not related to amplifier. It is pronounced AM-fuh-theater, NOT AMP-lih-theater.

Amputations   Many people who have suffered amputated limbs dislike the phrase "he lost his leg (or whatever)." They say, quite correctly, the leg is not lost at all, he knows exactly where he left it. The usage is so common, however, that it is probably acceptable.

Amuse/Bemuse   The most common usage of *AMUSE* is to mean to entertain or engage in a pleasurable pastime. *BEMUSE*, on the other hand means to confuse or bewilder. A less-used meaning is to cause to dream.

And Et Cetera   A redundancy. *ET* means *AND*. You shouldn't use et cetera in broadcast copy, anyhow. If there's more that the listeners should know, tell them.

Angina   Usually used to denote intense chest pain resulting from poorly circulating blood in the heart muscle. Medical people often pronounce it AN-jih-nuh. Most people say an-JY-nuh.

Angry/Mad Don't say *MAD* when you mean *ANGRY*. Mad means insane and some folks might just think LIBEL if you suggested they were mad.

Ante/Anti *ANTE* means to come before, antebellum—before the war, antediluvian—before the flood. Poker players ante up—place their money in the pot—before play begins. *ANTI* means acting against. "Antifreeze."

Antiseptic/Aseptic/Septic *ANTISEPTIC* (in its usual usage) refers to a substance that arrests or prevents the growth of bacteria. *ASEPTIC* means that the subject in question is free of bacteria. *SEPTIC* means it is contaminated.

Anxious/Eager Only in a minor way does *ANXIOUS* mean anything close to *EAGER*. Anxious indicates an element of worry or suspense—brooding fear. Eager means happy anticipation.

Anybody/Anyone. They mean the same thing, but use *ANYONE* for broadcast copy.

Anymore *ANYMORE* should be used only as a negative: "Sally doesn't live here anymore." The sense of the present time is nonstandard as in "We keep seeing the same birds anymore."

Appalachia That region of the Eastern U.S. mountain range which is viewed by some as severely affected by poverty, particularly in West Virginia, Kentucky and Tennessee. In these mountains the word is pronounced AP-uh-LATCH-uh, not AP-uh-LAY-chuh.

Appraise/Apprise *APPRAISE* usually means to set a value on something—real estate, auto damage. *APPRISE* also carries that notion in a rare usage. Most often, however, it means to inform.

Arctic/Antarctic These refer to the North and South Polar regions of the Earth. Mostly, note the spellings and pronunciations. It is ARK-tic and ANT-ark-tic.

Arthritis It is a painful disease that is pronounced arth-RYE-tiss. Only three syllables, note—it is not arth-ur-EYE-tiss.

Asian/Asiatic Use *ASIAN* when referring to the people of the region; use *ASIATIC* when referring to something to do with the Asian continent. There is some disagreement about this distinction—some authorities say Asiatic is derogatory.

As If/As Though/Like In most broadcast usage *AS IF* or *AS THOUGH* are equally acceptable. Do not use *LIKE* as a substitute.

Ascent/Assent *ASCENT* refers to rising upward, climbing. *ASSENT* means to agree to something.

Ascertain/Inquire To *ASCERTAIN* is to make certain of—to learn something. To *INQUIRE* is simply to ask about. One inquires in order to ascertain.

Assume/Presume *ASSUME* has many meanings; refer to a dictionary for a full discussion. Most often it is used to mean to take on—as an office—or to take for granted. *PRESUME* is very similar. It means to take upon one's self without authority, to expect or to accept as true without proof.

Astonish/Surprise The sense of *SURPRISE* in which we often use *ASTONISH* is one of its lesser meanings. Astonish has as its first meaning to stun as with great wonder. It also means to bewilder.

Attorney/Counsel/Lawyer There's a good deal of disagreement about the distinctions among these three words. Use *ATTORNEY* as a generic name for all persons who have been graduated from a law school. Use *COUNSEL* or *LAWYER* when referring to an attorney who is involved in a case. Use *COUNSEL* when the attorney is employed in some form other than general practice—such as a corporate counsel. Again, there's disagreement on this.

Audience/Spectators The crowd at a football game is not an *AUDIENCE* nor are the folks at a concert *SPECTATORS*. Look at the words. Audience has to do with hearing, and spectators with seeing. The primary role of the football fans is to see and the music lovers to listen, although some concerts today certainly have become spectacles. There are exceptions to these observations in common usage. *Television audience* for example, refers to TV viewers.

Aught/Ought Soundalikes   that   have   no   similarity   of meaning. *AUGHT* is an old word rarely used today. It means of little or no value, worthless, futile. It also means zero, cipher. *OUGHT* is an archaic past tense of the verb *to owe.* Today it is used to refer to an obligation. "A journalist ought to act responsibly."

Aunt　Depending on where you are, this female relative is pronounced either ANT or AWNT.

Author/Host　PLEASE, PLEASE, don't use these or similar nouns as verbs. Some language authorities are beginning to bend on this. Don't let them!

Automatic/Pistol/Revolver　There are two types of handguns— *AUTOMATICS* and *REVOLVERS.* They are both *PISTOLS* but they are not the same. A revolver has a cylinder which contains the cartridges, an automatic carries its ammunition in a clip, usually in the handle. The ammunition is referred to as rounds. The bullet is the projectile, the cartridge is the case which holds the bullet and powder. Handguns and rifles are measured in calibers —an expression of the diameter of the barrel. Shotguns are measured by gauge. Anyone who has served in the Army will tell you—perhaps in colorful terms—that a rifle is not a gun, it is a weapon.

Autopsy/Post Mortem　An *AUTOPSY* is a procedure performed on a dead person to determine the cause of death. It is therefore redundant to say "An autopsy will be performed to determine the cause of death." Avoid referring to an autopsy as a *POST MORTEM* even though it is performed after life ends. Post mortem is not a noun, it is an adjective describing when the procedure takes place. Autopsy, by the way, is pronounced AW-tup-see.

Baby/Infant/Toddler　Here we encounter the same problem we have with older children—what is the distinction we draw when we call a child a *BABY, INFANT,* or *TODDLER?* I believe a baby to be a newborn up to about six months, then the child becomes an infant until it begins to walk when it then becomes a toddler until about age three or four. This is strictly my opinion and is subject to challenge and change.

Badly   In the mistaken notion that it sounds "better" many people say they feel *BADLY* when they feel sick. That usage is British and is not considered standard American English. Here, we feel *BAD* when we're sick and feel *BADLY* when there's something wrong with our sense of touch. On the other hand, when we want something deeply, we correctly say "I want that badly."

Bail/Bale/Bond   *BAIL* and *BOND* differ in the source of the security. Bail is usually a sum of money or property posted by the accused privately, while bond is put up by a bondsman or some other institution. Both allow a prisoner to go free while awaiting trial or other legal procedure. Both are intended to assure the reappearance of the person in question. A *BALE* is a large bound bundle—among other things. One is not released "in lieu of bail." One is held in jail in lieu of bail. In lieu of means instead of.

Bait/Bate   A *BAIT* is something that might entice someone or some animal into a trap or onto a hook. *BATE* is from *abated* and means to restrain. The most common use is in the cliché "with bated breath," meaning anxious. To wait with bated breath means to be so anxious that one's breathing is in short gasps.

Baloney/Bologna   *BOLOGNA* is a common cold meat, and *BOLOGNA* is a city in Italy from which the cold meat takes its name. The city is pronounced buh-LOHN-yah. The meat is pronounced just like *BALONEY*, which is also a slang expression denoting disbelief.

Bank/Coast/Shore   Rivers and streams have *BANKS*, seas and oceans have *COASTS*, seas, oceans, lakes, and ponds have *SHORES*. Bank implies a steep slope, so it is possible for some lakes and ponds to have banks. However, when used as a general reference, use shore for lakes and ponds.

Base/Bass/Bass   A *BASE* is a footing, a foundation as well as a number of other things. In music, a *BASS* is pronounced BAYS (just like base) and means an instrument or voice of the low range. The fish, on the other hand, is pronounced BASS.

Basic/Bottom/Fundamental *BASIC* and *FUNDAMENTAL* are essentially synonyms referring to foundations or underlying principles. *BOTTOM* has some similar meanings, but most connote the underside of something and do not carry the idea of a foundation.

Bathing Suit The preferred reference (perhaps thanks to the Miss America folks) is *SWIMSUIT*.

Bazaar/Bizarre We all know this don't we? A *BAZAAR* is a fair or market place where a wide variety of goods is for sale. *BIZARRE* refers to erratic behavior or something or someone eccentric in style. There is a slight difference in pronunciation based on the initial vowel—buhz-AHR and bihz-AHR.

Beaufort Variously pronounced BOH-furt or BYOO-furt. Go with the flow—whatever the local pronunciation is, use it. The "Beaufort Scale" is a measure of wind velocity expressed as "Beaufort Force 0–12," with 0 being calm and 12 being hurricane force and above (plus 74 miles an hour).

Because/Since/Due To In broadcast copy prefer *BECAUSE*. *SINCE* can be confusing and *DUE TO* is pretentious.

Before/In Front of In one sense, *BEFORE* means *IN FRONT OF* as in "this program was taped before (in front of) a live audience." However, it is jarring to hear it reported that a witness appeared in front of a committee of Congress. To my ear, at least, the usage is substandard.

Bemuse *See* **Amuse**.

Be Sure To (And). Prefer *BE SURE TO. BE SURE AND* implies two actions. See also **Try And**.

Between *See* **Among**.

Biannual/Biennial *BI-ANNUAL* (it's best to hyphenate—see **Hyphens**) means occurring twice a year. *BI-ENNIAL* means occurring every two years.

Billion A thousand million. The British call it a *milliard*. Their *BILLION* is a thousand milliards.

Bisect/Dissect *BISECT* means to divide into two parts—usually equal. *DISSECT* (note spelling) can be pronounced either

DY-sect or dih-SECT depending on the construction of the sentence. It means—among other things—to divide into parts for study.

Bitter/Bitterly *See* **Weather Words.**

Blatant/Flagrant A *BLATANT* action would be one carried out in a noisy, offensive manner. A *FLAGRANT* action would be an evil or distastful one carried out in a conspicuous manner.

Blazed The Trail An axe mark on a tree is called a *BLAZE* and a series of them is used to mark trails through woods. The phrase does not have the sense of speed or intense activity. During a recent political campaign we saw this headline: "CANDIDATE BLAZES CAMPAIGN TRAIL." The story had to do with a day of intense activity. Wrong; the phrase may be used in the sense of breaking new ground, leading the way.

Bloc/Block A *BLOC* is a group of individuals or nations that have banded together to pursue a common purpose. The term is frequently (and almost exclusively) used to refer to political divisions (the Eastern Bloc nations). We all know the many meanings of *BLOCK*, don't we?

Boarder/Border A *BOARDER* is a person who takes meals regularly at a place away from home. He or she is not necessarily also lodging there. A *BORDER* is a boundary, usually between nations, among other things.

Boat/Ship A *BOAT* is a vessel small enough to be carried on a *SHIP*, but there are numerous exceptions—tug boat, for example.

Boor/Bore A *BOOR* is a lout, someone uncouth in manners or insensitive. A *BORE* (when referring to persons or situations) is someone or something that is uninteresting, dull. Bore, of course, has many other meanings.

Bouillon/Bullion *BOUILLON* is a thin, clear soup usually made from chicken or beef stock. *BULLION* is metal in a mass. It can be any metal, but usually refers to gold or silver in ingots, most often gold. It is not redundant to refer to "gold bullion."

Boy Friend/Girl Friend Neither of these phrases should be applied to adults, except in a facetious manner, or in a gossip column.

Boy/Man   Somewhere back in the 1960s we lost track of when a *BOY* becomes a *MAN*. It probably had to do with the lowering of the voting and drinking ages. We have since seen such absurdities as a lead saying "Two county men drowned today in Smith Pond," only to read that one was 19 and the other 14! Let's settle on 18 as the age when man- and womanhood occurs. A preteen male is referred to as a boy, 13 through 17 he is a youth, after that he becomes a man. We don't have an equivalent word to youth for teenage girls, so use girl until age 18, then woman. If married, no matter how young, use man and woman. Some authorities say youth is a genderless word and applies to both teenage boys and girls. I have always thought of it as a male term.

Brackish   Maybe I'm the only person who reached mid-life believing that *BRACKISH* meant muddy or polluted. It doesn't, of course. It means somewhat salty—less so than sea water—but still undrinkable. The word has been used to mean unpalatable. Brackish water occurs where the sea enters a river or bay and meets fresh water flowing out. Certain marine life, such as the blue crab, needs brackish water at certain times of the year. See how much you can learn just by reading a silly word guide?

Brassiere/Brazier   You can get yourself terribly embarrassed by confusing these two. The women's undergarment is correctly pronounced bra-zee-AIR. However, it is usually pronounced bruh-ZEER and ordinarily shortened to BRA. A *BRAZIER* on the other hand, is a fire pit, such as an outdoor barbeque grill. It is pronounced BRAY-zhur.

Breach/Breech/Broach/Brook   Here we have a group of almost-soundalikes that are easily confused. A *BREACH* is a violation—breach of contract, or a gap such as a breach in a dam. *BREECH* is the lower part of the human torso, hence "breeches" (pronounced BRITCH-ez); it is also that part of a rifle or cannon that receives the ammunition, which is pronounced BREECH. *BROACH* most often means to bring up a subject; it is also a nautical term for a very dangerous situation in which a sailing vessel veers broadside to the wind and waves. *BROOK* aside from being a small stream, means to tolerate—to put up with. It is usually used in the negative sense: "The Governor will brook no criticism."

Bring/Take   One *BRINGS* something here and *TAKES* something there. That's pretty simple, so why do we keep hearing "Bring this to Uncle Charlie in Baltimore?"

Broad/Wide   Yes, there's a difference. *WIDE* generally refers to the distance that separates two implied boundaries—a wide river. *BROAD* is a reference to what lies between the limits—a broad field. The words are often used interchangably, especially in colloquial expressions such as "wide-eyed" or broad daylight.

Broken Bones   Don't write "He broke his arm." That implies he somehow deliberately broke the bone. It would be a very unusual story indeed if someone purposely broke a bone.

Bullet   *See* **Automatic**.

Bulletin   *See* **Wire Services**.

Burgeon   To sprout or flourish (pronounced BUHR-jahn): There is the sense of sudden and widespread growth. We speak of a burgeoning city.

Burglary/Robbery   A *ROBBERY* is the taking of another's property through threat or violence. Thus, an empty house is not robbed, but *BURGLARIZED* which has the sense of breaking-in and stealing built in.

Bury   Watch the pronunciation. It is BURR-ee, not BAIR-ee.

Bus/Buss   A *BUS* is a vehicle. The word is derived from omnibus which is what the British call their public transport. The plural is buses. A *BUSS* is a kiss, usually with the sense of a sudden, impulsive show of affection.

Bust   The use is sufficiently widespread that we can accept the slang *DRUG BUST*.

Cache/Cash   Yes, you can have a *CACHE* of *CASH*. A cache is a hiding place and, by extension, what is hidden there. It is pronounced just like cash.

Caliber/Gauge   *See* **Automatic**.

Callous/Callus   Both words have the meaning of hardened or thickened skin, but CALLOUS also means to be insensitive and unsympathetic. They are both pronounced the same: KAL-us.

Calvary/Cavalry   Some people seem to be incapable of uttering *CAVALRY* and will almost always say *CALVARY* instead. Calvary is a hill near Jerusalem where Jesus is believed to have been crucified. The cavalry used to be horse-mounted troops and today the word is sometimes used to refer to motorized military units.

Canada   *See* **America**.

Canada Goose   The bird is a *CANADA GOOSE* not a *Canadian Goose*.

Cancel Out   *OUT* is unnecessary. The idea is built into *CANCEL*.

Can/May   Easily and often misused. Use *CAN* when your sense is "is able to," use *MAY* when the sense is "has permission to." Both words have other uses and senses, but the mix-up occurs between ability and permission.

Cannon/Canon   A *CANNON* is a field weapon, as we all know. A *CANON* is a law or rule, usually having to do with the practice of religion. However, some secular organizations have codified their rules of conduct into what they call canons.

Canuck   A disparaging term for a Canadian, especially a French Canadian. Even though they, themselves, may use the term—even naming a hockey team the "Canucks"—it is still a term many Canadians find offensive.

Canvas/Canvass   Both pronounced the same—KAN-vus. *CANVAS* is a heavy cloth, usually cotton, used to make tents, tarpaulins and, in the old days, sails. A *CANVASS* is a poll or survey. A few days following an election, there is conducted what is known as the official canvass, in which election officials examine and certify the results.

Capacity   *See* **Ability**.

Capital/Capitol   The city and the money are the *CAPITAL*. The building is the *CAPITOL*, both national and state. Capital, used in the sense of a crime punishable by death, comes from the Latin for head.

Carat/Caret/Carrot/Karat   Here we have another group of soundalikes. A *CARAT* is a measure of weight of precious stones or metals. *KARAT* means about the same thing, but is usually reserved for gold. A *CARET* is a proof-reader's pointed mark indicating where material is to be inserted in a page of copy, like this^. Of course you know what a *CARROT* is.

Careen/Career   *CAREEN* and *CAREER* share one meaning—that of lurching. But they both have more common use. *CAREEN* is the act of beaching a boat where it will tilt to one side at low tide so that work can be done on the bottom below the waterline. The most common use of *CAREER* is to refer to one's employment or course through life. It has several other meanings as well, most having to do with short bursts of speed, as in a horse race.

Caribbean   The Sea is pronounced kahr-uh-BEE-un or kah-RIB-ean. Some dictionaries prefer the latter, I prefer the former. The Caribbean Sea, by the way, lies to the south of Cuba and north of South America. It is bounded on the East by the Leeward and Windward Islands. The Gulf of Mexico is not included.

Carpet/Rug   Modern usage, unsupported by Webster's, has *CARPET* meaning wall-to-wall floor covering, and other floor coverings referred to as *RUGS*. This is an area of disagreement. After all, the "Magic Carpet" was a rug.

Cartridge   *See* **Automatic**.

Caster/Castor   In the usual sense, *CASTER* refers to a swiveled wheel on furniture, but it does have other meanings. *CASTOR* is most familiar as "castor oil." It, too, has other meanings, including the name of one of two bright stars in the constellation Gemini.

Casual/Causal   Mostly, be careful with the spellings and be sure to clearly mark your copy if you expect to have *CAUSAL* pronounced correctly on the air. A casual relationship and a causal relationship are two very different things! It is best to avoid *causal*.

Casualty/Death   *CASUALTY* should be reserved for the victims of war or disaster. All casualties are not dead—they include injured, wounded, missing, and any others who may be lost to a military command for whatever reason other than leave. It may be clever to refer to a former officeholder as a casualty of an election, but it is not accurate and can mislead an audience that may not be listening closely.

Catsup/Ketchup They are both pronounced KEH-chup and so is *catch up* which we sometimes see. For broadcast scripts, use the spelling *ketchup*.

Celebrant/Celebrator It is good to draw the distinction. *CELEBRANT* usually refers to a person performing a public religious ceremony, especially in the Catholic church. A *CELEBRATOR* is simply one taking part in a celebration of whatever nature.

Cement/Concrete *CEMENT* (pronounced sih-MENT) is only one ingredient in *CONCRETE*, which also contains water, sand gravel, or some other aggregate. Once mixed, it is concrete. Therefore that big mixer truck is a concrete truck, not a cement truck. The same is true of the mixer at a construction site—it is a concrete mixer, not a cement mixer.

Censer/Censor/Censure/Sensor A *CENSER* is an incense burner such as is used in certain religious ceremonies. We all know what a *CENSOR* is, don't we? The person who, sometimes officially, but often not, checks various forms of communication for materials deemed unfit for the public. To *CENSURE* is to officially reprimand or disapprove. A *SENSOR* is a device, usually electronic, that senses operating conditions of various machines and other things and sends impulses to control units or alarms.

Center On/Revolve Around Think about it. You cannot *CENTER* around something.

Chair A *CHAIR* is a piece of furniture intended for sitting upon. The word should not be used to indicate the person who presides at a meeting, the head of a committee or any other such thing. It has come into use to avoid what some perceive to be the sexist "chairman." If the honcho happens to be a woman, call her a "chairwoman." Yes, Webster almost says *chair* is an adjective for a person presiding over a meeting. Here's one place we diverge. I think its use in that sense is confusing.

Chaise Longue   Note the spelling. It is NOT a *lounge*. We can get fairly close to the French pronunciation with SHAYZ LAWNG. Literally, it means "long chair." Webster accepts chaise lounge as a secondary pronunciation. It's another of those foreign terms that has been halfway absorbed into English. Petit fours is another.

Champagne/Champaign/Champlain   *CHAMPAGNE* is the sparkling white wine originally from the Champagne region of France. A *CHAMPAIGN* is a broad open field, hence the name of the Illinois city. *CHAMPLAIN* is the lake that forms most of the border between Vermont and New York state.

Chargé D'Affaires   A member of a diplomatic mission or embassy who ranks below the person in charge, but acts in his or her behalf in his or her absence or at certain ceremonies. The term is pronounced shar-ZHAY duh-FAIR.

Chic   Pronounced SHEEK, regardless of what the jeans maker tells us.

Chicano   An American of Mexican origin, also applied to illegal aliens from south of the border. It does not apply to all people with Spanish surnames. Pronounce it chih-KAWN-oh.

Childish/Childlike   *CHILDISH* behavior is immature. The term is usually used as a criticism. *CHILDLIKE* is used, on the other hand, to imply innocence or playfulness and is most often used as a compliment.

Chile/Chili/Chilly   All are pronounced *CHILLY*. *CHILE* is a country in South America. CHILI is a spicy bean dish. When meat is added, it becomes "chili con carne."

China   There are two. The People's Republic of China, on the mainland and the Republic of China established following World War II on the island of Taiwan (formerly Formosa). Neither cares to be confused with the other.

Choral/Chorale/Coral   *CHORAL* and *CHORALE* both refer to music. Choral is a kind of music written to be sung by a chorus or choir. A chorale is the performance of a chorus. Choral and *CORAL*—the tiny marine animals—are both pronounced KOH-rul. *Chorale* is pronounced koh-RALL, just like the horse pen, corral.

Chord/Cord   *CHORD* is chiefly a reference to a musical sound, but the word also has meanings in geometry and construction. A *CORD* is either a length of line somewhere between a string and a rope or a stack of fire wood four feet wide, four feet high and eight feet long. It has many other meanings, as well, including a kind of fabric and the nerve bundle in the spine.

Christmas Eve   It used to be that *CHRISTMAS EVE* was the night before Christmas. It seems now, however, that all of December 24th is referred to as Christmas Eve. The same applies to New Year's Eve as well.

Cite/Sight/Site   To *CITE* is to call attention to, especially some quoted material brought out as evidence. *SIGHT*, of course, has to do with vision or seeing. A *SITE* is a location; we speak of a building site.

Clambered/Clamored   Both pronounced CLAM-urd. *CLAMBERED* refers to climbing, usually in an awkward or hurried fashion. *CLAMORED* has to do with insistently making noise—the cat clamored for its food.

Clapboard   A type of building siding. The preferred pronunciation is KLAB-urd, just like sour milk.

Clean/Cleanse   Perhaps soap commercials have caused this problem. Both *CLEAN* and *CLEANSE* (pronounced KLENZ) mean to rid of soil, but in different ways. *Clean* has to do with removing physical dirt. *Cleanse* has to do with spiritual matters—"cleansing" one's self of guilt, for example. Wouldn't it be wonderful if we really could buy a "cleanser" in a box at the grocery store?

Cleave   One of the little tricks English plays on us from time to time. *CLEAVE* has two directly opposing meanings. In one sense it means to split apart—hence meat cleaver. Its other sense is to cling together—to be loyal. Some marriage rites use the term to describe the bond between husband and wife. It's fortunate the word is not commonly used. I would not suggest it as a good broadcast word.

Clench/Clinch   *CLENCH* is to close tightly, as your fist or jaw. *CLINCH* means to secure firmly—we speak of clinching the end of a nail by bending it over so it cannot be pulled out. It is used quite correctly in saying "the team clinched the title," but in that use it is a cliché.

Client/Customer/Patron   We generally think of a *CLIENT* as one who seeks personal help from a professional, such as a lawyer, although the word does have broader meaning, including persons who are served by social agencies. *CUSTOMERS* are found in stores and other businesses and the word is also used to describe those who purchase various services. *PATRON*, on the other hand, is a confused word. It means one who supports and is also used to denote one who is served. It is best not to use patron when you mean client or customer.

Climactic/Climatic   *CLIMACTIC* refers to the climax, usually accompanied by "moment," of a novel, play or any other activity that builds toward a high point. *CLIMATIC* refers to climate—the weather.

Clique   Pronounced KLEEK. It means a close (often closed) group.

Close Proximity   A redundancy. If something is proximate, it is close.

Coincident/Simultaneous   Both words mean occurring or existing at the same time, but, *COINCIDENT* is a much broader term. *SIMULTANEOUS* has to do only with time. When two things arrive at exactly the same moment they are said to be simultaneous. A coincidence can involve things that take place at the same time, or in the same place, or under the same circumstances.

Cole Slaw and the Rest of the Menu   How many menus have you seen—usually hand-lettered but sometimes elaborately printed—that say you may have COLD SLAW, ICE TEA, TOSS SALAD, CORN BEEF, GRILL CHEESE, all done up in WAXED PAPER? They are all wrong, of course. It is COLE, ICED, TOSSED, CORNED, GRILLED AND WAX. Menu editing can be a great pastime while waiting for service.

College/University   The most common usage in the United States has *COLLEGE* meaning an institution of higher learning that offers courses leading to the bachelor's degree. A *UNIVERSITY* is often made up of colleges and offers educational programs at the Master's or Doctoral level.

Collision   There is some shifting from the original usage of

COLLISION. Purists (myself included on this one) insist that a collision is the violent coming together of two moving objects. Therefore, an automobile cannot "collide" with a tree. Recently, some wordsmiths have been saying that sticking to that narrow meaning of the word is sophistry.

Collusion/Connivance *COLLUSION* is a secret agreement formed for the purpose of deceiving someone not in on the secret. *CONNIVANCE* is the intentional ignoring of wrongdoing or the condoning of wrongdoing.

Commitment/Committal *COMMITMENT* and *COMMITTAL* (note spellings) have numerous meanings, but they are quite distinct in their most common uses: *commitment* has to do with emotional attachment, being pledged; *committal* is the act (usually legal) of consigning one to prison or a mental institution. The hearing in such cases is called a committal hearing, not a commitment hearing. We also speak of a committal service when burying the dead.

Comparable Often mispronounced. It is KAWM-pur-uh-buhl.

Communique The French word is frequently used to describe a statement issued following diplomatic talks. It can mean any formal message. It is pronounced kuh-myoon-ih-KAY.

Complacent/Complaisant *COMPLACENT* means self-satisfied, even smug, about one's accomplishments or place. It is not always a complimentary term. *COMPLAISANT* has to do with a willingness to be pleasant or to serve, sometimes in a fawning manner. Again, not always complimentary.

Complected/Complexioned Use *COMPLEXIONED* when referring to skin color. *COMPLECTED* is not widely accepted as standard usage.

Complement/Compliment There is a tiny difference in the pronunciation of these two, as well as huge differences in meaning. *COMPLEMENT* (pronounced KOM-pleh-ment) means to make complete, but in common usage it has come to mean something that enhances, such as "her make-up complements her dress." A *COMPLIMENT* (pronounced KOM-plih-ment) is an expression of approval or praise.

Compose/Comprise These are frequently confused, and often can be used interchangeably. But, they are distinct. *COMPOSE* means to combine things, "Ninety-eight counties compose Virginia." *COMPRISE* means to be made up of: "Virginia comprises ninety-eight counties." It might help to think of it this way: *compose* starts with the parts and makes up the whole, while *comprise* starts with the whole and discusses the parts. Another point is that *comprise* should never be used with "of," but "composed of" is entirely correct.

Comptroller I don't care how it's spelled, it's pronounced "controller." *COMPTROLLERS* are found in business, industry, and government. They are the keepers of accounts—super accountants, if you will—who often have the authority to determine whether expenditures are appropriate.

Conclave Originally, a term for secret meetings of religious organizations. The meeting of cardinals to select a new Roman Catholic pope is still called a *CONCLAVE*. It has also come to mean any secret or closed assembly.

Concrete *See* **Cement**.

Confidant/Confident A *CONFIDANT* (pronounced KAWN-fih-DAHNT) is a person in whom secrets are confided and entrusted. To be *CONFIDENT* (pronounced KAWN-fih-dent) is to be self-assured and free of worry.

Consecutive/Successive *CONSECUTIVE* means one-after-another, a continuous progression. *SUCCESSIVE* has a similar meaning, but also a number of others having to do with lines of inheritance. Be careful which you use to avoid confusion.

Consequent/Subsequent *CONSEQUENT* means to follow as the result of some prior happening. *SUBSEQUENT* is a broader word, meaning to follow at a later time, but not necessarily as the result of something earlier.

Console/Console To *CONSOLE* (pronounced kuhn-SOHL and KAWN-sohl) someone is to offer sympathy or comfort, usually emotional support. A *CONSOLE* is a variety of things, but to broadcasters it generally refers to audio and video control panels in the (where else?) control room.

Contagious/Infectious *CONTAGIOUS* means communicable by contact—catching. It can also have a subtler meaning, as in "her happiness was contagious." *INFECTIOUS* (note spelling) means capable of causing infection. It also has the emotional use: "His laugh was infectious."

Contemporary *CONTEMPORARY* is not a synonym for modern in its primary sense. Contemporary means living or existing at the same time. Jefferson and Washington were contemporaries. The word is used to describe modern—often unconventional—styles of homes or furnishings. The usage is confusing and should be avoided.

Contentious/Controversial A *CONTENTIOUS* person is one given to quarrels. It is proper to refer to a person as being *CONTROVERSIAL*, but that means the person is an object of controversy. The usual sense has to do with issues. In broadcasting we have to worry about "controversial issues of public importance" in dealing with the Fairness Doctrine.

Contiguous *See* **Adjacent**.

Continual/Continuous The ticking of a clock is a *CONTINUAL* sound, as is the fall of a trip-hammer. The flow of a river is *CONTINUOUS*—going on without interruption.

Convict/Inmate/Prisoner Be careful here. The key point is that not everyone in jail is a *CONVICT*; many are being held for trial or other action and have not been convicted of anything. You can be assured that everyone in a state or federal penitentiary is a convict. It is best to refer to all folks in a local jail as *PRISONERS*. They are all *INMATES*, no matter where they are locked up.

Cooperate It is a common redundancy to say "cooperate together." *COOPERATE* means just that—operate together.

Copter Do not use as a verb: "He coptered to New York."

Copy/Replica This may be a lost cause. A *COPY* of the Mayflower is not a *REPLICA*. To be a true replica, an object must be a copy of an original done by the same artist, or under his or her supervision.

Coronary/Heart Attack   Informally, a *HEART ATTACK* is often referred to as a *CORONARY*. Technically—and correctly—coronary refers to the arteries of the heart that might become obstructed, resulting in a heart attack. One should not refer to a heart attack as a coronary. It might be a *coronary occlusion* or a *coronary thrombosis* which are specific kinds of heart attacks. Please do not refer to a *massive heart attack* unless you are quoting medical authority. From the standpoint of the victim, most heart attacks are massive.

Coroner/Medical Examiner/Pathologist   A *CORONER* is not necessarily a medical doctor. A coroner is a public official—often elected—whose duty it is to investigate any death deemed to be of other than natural causes. A *MEDICAL EXAMINER*, on the other hand, usually is a medical doctor, usually appointed, whose duties are similar to those of a "coroner." The title varies by locality or state. Autopsies (see **AUTOPSY**) are conducted by *PATHO-LOGISTS* who are medical doctors and may or may not be appointed medical examiners. A medical examiner or a coroner may call an inquest to investigate a suspicious death. A special coroner's jury is impanelled to carry out the investigation. The jury recommends whether a police investigation should be conducted.

Corporation/Incorporated   Do not use *incorporation* as part of the name of a company. It is either *CORPORATION* or "INCORPORATED." *Incorporation* is the act of incorporating.

Corps   Pronounce it KOR. It's one of those rarities where two consonants are silent.

Could Not Have Cared Less   The phrase "I could have cared less" came into the idiom (or at least came to my attention) in the early 1960s. What is meant of course, is *I COULD NOT HAVE CARED LESS*. The origin of this nonsense is a mystery to me. I thought it may have been passing out of use, but I keep hearing it—most recently in a formal speech before a distinguished university audience from the lips of an undeservedly revered newspaper executive.

Counsel   *See* **Attorney**.

Country/Nation   *COUNTRY* is a much broader concept than *NATION*. *Nation* usually refers to an independent state, while *country* can be a regional concept. Generally the words are considered synonymous.

Coup De Grace   Pronounced Kood-eh-GRAHS. A death blow, usually meant to end the suffering of a wounded enemy or animal. It also is used symbolically to refer to the final act that ends a regime or idea of long standing.

Coup D'Etat   Pronounced Kood-eh-TAH. It is the violent overthrow of a government, usually by the military. *Coup* means *stroke*, so a *coup d'etat* is a stroke against the state.

Couple   A collective noun that is to be treated as a singular in most cases. However, see the earlier discussion of collectives, where you will find advice not to drag the singular treatment on to nonsense.

Craps   The game played with dice is *CRAPS*. Always expressed as a plural. *Crap* is something else entirely.

Credible/Creditable/Credulous   Very closely similar and easily confused are *CREDIBLE, CREDITABLE,* and *CREDULOUS*. Journalists place great value on being credible, like to be creditable, and hope to Heaven they are not credulous. *Credible* means believable, reliable; *creditable* has a similar meaning in an older, rarely used obsolete sense in which credit means to believe, but in modern use it means commendable, trustworthy; *credulous* means to be easily fooled, gullible, ready to believe without proof.

Creditor/Debtor   A *CREDITOR* is someone to whom something, usually money, is owed. A *DEBTOR* is someone who owes, again, usually money.

Cue/Queue   Both pronounced KEW. A *CUE* can be a number of things, a pool cue, an actor's entrance line and so on. A *QUEUE* is usually a waiting line, but can also refer to a braid of hair hanging down the back.

Currently/Presently   *CURRENTLY* and *PRESENTLY* are not synonymous. "The temperature is presently 60 degrees," is not literate. *Currently* means right now, *presently* means soon, in a short time. "He will arrive presently." I think the problem here stems from "present" meaning right now. The "ly" gets tacked on because it "sounds better." Webster's approves, but I have reservations.

Cyclone/Hurricane/Tornado/Typhoon A *CYCLONE* is a circular motion of wind around an atmospheric low pressure area. It is usually characterized by moderate winds and precipitation. It is not necessarily a damaging storm and it is not a synonym for *TORNADO*. A *HURRICANE* is a widespread intense cyclone in which sustained winds have exceeded 74 miles an hour. A *TORNADO* is an intense cyclone over land (over water it is called a *water spout*) characterized by a funnel-shaped cloud and accompanied by heavy rain; it is very dangerous storm. A *TYPHOON* is an intense cyclone occurring in the area of the China Sea. It is what we call a hurricane.

Cynic/Skeptic Both words derive from ancient schools of philosophy. A *CYNIC* is a person who believes or expresses the opinion that human conduct is motivated primarily by self-interest. A *SKEPTIC* is a doubtful person, one who believes that some knowledge is unknowable.

Dairy/Diary Be careful with the spellings. If the construction of your sentence could cause confusion for your anchor, then mark your copy to make sure the right word is used.

Dais/Lectern/Podium *DAIS* and *PODIUM* are the same things. Either is a proper name for a raised platform on which a speaker, for example, stands before an audience. Take your pick, but podium is the more familiar. A *LECTERN* (note spelling) is a stand or box with a sloping top on which a speaker places his or her script.

Damaged/Injured/Wounded *DAMAGE* occurs only to inanimate objects. You are *INJURED* in an accident, but *WOUNDED* by a weapon. In medical circles many injuries, including surgical incisions, are referred to as wounds. A wound must penetrate the skin.

Damper/Draft The *DAMPER* on a wood stove or fireplace is the device used to control the *DRAFT*. A favorite "fool's errand" on which to send an apprentice boilermaker in the old days was to ask him to go back to the shop to get the draft for the furnace. The draft is the air flow through the fire box, controlled by the damper.

Data/Datum   We may be witnessing the death of a word. *DATA* is plural, the singular is *DATUM*. Correct usage is "data are..." It sounds awkward to many people and we hear data used as a singular more and more frequently. I still treat it as a plural, and I think you should too.

Deaf Mute   A *DEAF MUTE* is a person who lacks both a full sense of hearing and the ability to speak. Not all deaf people are mutes. Avoid *deaf and dumb*, which in the insensitive days of the past was used for deaf mute. It is now considered derogatory.

Deaths   Be careful of the pronunciation of the plural. There is no really good way to write a phonetic for the TH sound, which differs from the sound of Smith and that of although. The plural of death should sound like Smith's.

Debtor   *See* **Creditor**.

Debut/Debuted   A *DEBUT* (pronounced day-BYOO) once meant specifically the introduction to society, or the introduction of a new performer or performance. It has come into much broader use in recent times, but still carries the idea of an introduction to the public. There is no such word as debuted, which we often see as the past tense of debut. If you write that in broadcast copy, you'll get *de-butted*. *Debut* is a noun—therefore, it has no past tense.

Decade/Decayed   The difference in pronunciation here is the problem. *DECADE* is pronounced DECK-aid. *DECAYED* is pronounced duh-KAYED. Many words that begin with de- have the initial syllable pronounced as duh. Avoid hitting a stressed DEE sound.

Decimate   In the bad old days, Roman soldiers followed the quaint practice of *DECIMATING* a defeated army. That meant to go through the ranks and kill every tenth man. *Decimate* means to reduce by one-tenth. However, the word has come to mean the destruction of a considerable part of something. Be careful in its use; avoid saying "The

Yankees decimated the Red Sox," particularly if you live in Boston.

Declaim/Disclaim   *DECLAIM* means to speak pompously or rhetorically as one might in an elocution exercise. *DISCLAIM* means to deny a connection with something. A disclaimer is often used in broadcasting to notify the listener that an opinion expressed on the air is not necessarily shared by the station or its employees.

Decorum   *DECORUM*, by definition, refers to good behavior. "Correct decorum" is a redundancy.

Degree/Diploma   You earn a *DEGREE* and it is conferred upon you by an institution of higher learning (high schools do not confer degrees). Usually, you are handed a *DIPLOMA* to hang on your wall to proclaim to the world that you earned the degree. A *degree* is a rank, a *diploma* is a document.

Demur/Demure   *DEMUR* is a term used chiefly in legal matters, the action being known as a *demurrer*. It means to object to something, to take exception to. *DEMURE* means to be modest, perhaps even being affectedly reserved. To me it has always also had the connotation of referring to a small, young woman.

Despite/In Spite Of   Both are used to mean notwithstanding. *DESPITE*, however, has a number of other meanings, all having to do with spiteful behavior. Use *in spite of.*

Destroyed   To say something is "totally destroyed" is a redundancy. Destruction is, by definition, complete. We, of course, frequently hear the expression "partially destroyed." What is meant is *damaged.*

Detroit/Tennessee/Vermont   All frequently mispronounced by stressing the first syllables. It is dee-TROIT, ten-uh-SEE (with light stress on the ten) and ver-MAWNT.

Diagnosis/Prognosis   *DIAGNOSIS* in medical usage is the process of identifying a disease by its signs and symptoms. The word has come into use by auto mechanics and computer operators, among others—but still means about the same thing. A *PROGNOSIS* is a prediction of the course of and result of an illness. It, too, is used in other contexts. Weather people speak of *progging* the weather

—forecasting. Please, let us not. It is Weather Service jargon.

Die from/Die of   We *DIE OF* a disease or accident, we do not *DIE FROM* such causes, or any others for that matter.

Die/Perish   In *A Dictionary of Euphemisms and Other Double-talk*, Hugh Rawson offers an excellent catalogue of the many ways English-speakers refer to death without actually saying it. There seem to be scores (maybe hundreds) of such euphemisms, but *PERISH* is not one of them. In common use, perish carries the sense of slow death, such as from freezing. Vegetables are said to be "perishable" because they will slowly decay. I don't think it would be advisable to refer to a traffic fatality as having perished. However, I think people perish in fires.

Different from/Different than   It is *DIFFERENT FROM* no matter how many extra words it takes to use that form. *DIFFERENT THAN* is nonstandard, at best. Webster's doesn't object.

Diffident/Indifferent   *DIFFIDENT* is much like reticent. It means to be reluctant to speak because of shyness or fear of being wrong. It can also apply to action—which reticent cannot. INDIFFERENT means to be neutral—neither one side nor the other. It can also mean uncaring, uninvolved. We say a person received an indifferent education, meaning the teachers really didn't care what sort of education their students received.

Dilemma   Here's another of those words with a built-in sense of number. A *DILEMMA* (note spelling) is a problem with two possible courses of action—both of them undesirable. That's what a dilemma is and nothing else.

Diminish/Minimize   *DIMINISH* means to reduce in size or quantity, but not to any particular degree. To *MINIMIZE* means to reduce as far as possible—to the minimum.

Diphtheria/Diphthong/Naphtha   Note the spellings. These words all contain the "PHTH" combination of consonants, and, yes, they are pronounced: diff-THER-ee-a, DIFF-thong, NAFF-tha. No matter how many years you have been saying and hearing others say DIPP-theria and NAP-tha, it's not the preferred pronunciation. Hardly anyone ever says diphthong, right or wrong.

Disburse/Disperse These two almost sound-alikes need careful pronunciation. To *DISBURSE* is to make payments, to distribute the proceeds of, for example, a will. To *DISPERSE* is to scatter or spread about. It also can mean to evaporate.

Discomfit/Discomfort *DISCOMFIT* is another bad broadcast word because it sounds so much like *DISCOMFORT*. *Discomfit* means to disconcert or embarrass. *DISCOMFORT* can mean being uncomfortable in any way, not just through embarrassment.

Discover/Invent *DISCOVER* is sometimes mistakenly used when the writer wants *INVENT*. It is correct to say Madame Curie "discovered" radium. She uncovered something that was already there, but unknown. To invent means to create something that had not previously existed. Alexander Graham Bell, it is said, "invented" the telephone.

Discreet/Discrete These words are so frequently confused in the spelling that it appears not many writers know the difference. *DISCREET* has to do with behavior that is circumspect, not showy; prudent, cautious. *DISCRETE* refers to something or someone that is separate and identifiable as an entity. Something can be made up of discrete parts.

Disinterested/Uninterested *DISINTERESTED* means neutral, as a judge is expected to be, taking no sides. *UNINTERESTED* means having no interest in something, paying no attention.

Dissect *See* **Bisect**.

Dissemble/Assemble We all know that *ASSEMBLE* means to bring together things or people. *DISSEMBLE* means to deceive in a subtle way, to overlook or ignore facts contrary to the impression desired. It's a bad broadcast word.

Dock/Pier/Wharf These words have been so thoroughly confused over so many years, there's probably no point in trying to unscramble them. But, *DOCK* is a place in which a ship is moored—the watery space between piers, for example. The expression "come to dock" probably has led to the use of *dock* to mean the *PIER*. *Dock* takes up more than a full dictionary column with its many and varied meanings. A *pier* (note spelling) and a *WHARF* (the "h" is silent) are about the same thing—a structure extending out from shore against which a ship may lie while moored. I think most people would think of passengers when one says *pier* and of cargo at the word *wharf*. Maybe not.

Dog-Eared   We are usually referring to the condition of a book when we say something is *DOG-EARED*. It refers to the practice of turning down a corner of a page to mark a place, folding the paper to resemble the ear of certain dogs. However, the phrase has come to mean shabby, worn or beat-up.

Down East   Applies only to Maine; and in Maine, only to the coastal area.

Down Under   Refers only to Australia and New Zealand. The reference is to their location south of the Equator.

Draft/Draught/Drought   *DRAFT* and *DRAUGHT* are both pronounced *DRAFT*. And, in referring to drinking, share identical meanings. *Draught* is principally a British usage. *Draft* has numerous other meanings, mostly having to do with drawing, either on paper, or on a rope. Draft also, of course, means the drawing of lots as in military conscription. *DROUGHT* refers to a prolonged period of shortage—usually of water. It is pronounced DROWT—rhymes with TROUT. Sometimes, but rarely, you will see it spelled *DROUTH* but the pronunciation remains the same.

Dreamed/Dreamt   Both are the past tense of "dream." Use *DREAMT* for broadcast use; *DREAMED* sounds awful.

Drowned   Do not precede with the verb *was*. That implies action by an outside force. "He was drowned by his wife" is correct usage. But, if he fell off the boat and didn't come up, he drowned.

Drugs/Medicine/Medication   Be careful, in this day and time, of the use of the word *DRUGS*. There was a time when to say a person was taking drugs simply meant he was taking medicine; no more. *MEDICATION* is just a fancy word for *MEDICINE*. Use *medicine*.

Drunk/Drunken   A person may be drunk but is arrested for drunken driving. *DRUNK* is a state of being, *DRUNKEN* is the adjective for actions while drunk.

Dual/Duel   Careful pronunciation will distinguish these words for your listeners. *DUAL* has to do with two's...the dual wheels on a truck, for example. A *DUEL* is a fight, usually with weapons, between two contestants. Note the notion of there being only two participants is built in. When duelling was accepted, it was usually a formal combat before witnesses. Today we use the term more metaphorically in speaking of contests between opposing persons, ideas, theories or banjos.

Due To   *See* **Because**.

Dwell/Live/Reside   *DWELL* is quaint. *RESIDE* is stilted. Use *LIVE*.

Each/Either   Any time you're tempted to use *EITHER* (pronounced, please, EE-thur) stop and think. It is perfectly correct to say "take either route." However, it is wrong to say "the flowers are on either end of the coffin." What you want in that phrase is *EACH*. Either carries the notion of choice.

Eager   *See* **Anxious**.

Earthquake/Richter Scale/Temblor   We all know what an *EARTHQUAKE* is, but many of us aren't too sure about the *RICHTER* (pronounced RIK-tur) *SCALE*, or so it would seem from stories I have read telling me that the scale is a 10-point system for measuring the severity of an earthquake. In fact, there is no top limit on the Richter scale. Geologists tell me that 9 is the theoretical maximum, because beyond that everything would be destroyed. The scale is set up so that 4 is not just double 2, it is four times. So, by the time you get to 9, it's all over. Note the spelling and pronunciation of *TEMBLOR*. That is the term for the actual shaking of an earthquake. It is pronounced just as it is spelled: TEM-blur. It, however, is a weird word and *trembler* or even *tremor* are acceptable and certainly more understandable.

Ecology/Environment   Don't get these words mixed up. Actually nearly everyone has had them confused for 20 years, but there's no reason to perpetuate the confusion. The *ENVIRONMENT* is just a part of *ECOLOGY*. Ecology is the study of the inter-relationship of organisms and their environment. The environment is the surrounding conditions that influence the ecology. It's eh-KOL-oh-gee by the way.

Effect   *See* **Affect.**

Effete/Elite   Here we have a real misunderstanding. *EFFETE* means burned out, decadent, having lost stamina as a result of overrefinement or lax standards. ELITE refers to the choice part, the cream of the crop. Effete was given new life by Spiro Agnew's speech writer in 1969; let's forget it.

Effluent   *See* **Affluent.**

Eject/Evict   A person who is, through legal process, EVICTED from his or her home, in fact is also EJECTED. But the relationship of the two words in common use does not go the other direction. A person ejected from a restaurant, for example, should not be said to have been evicted. The idea of legal process in built into *evict*, but not *eject*.

Elder/Older   Dictionaries tell us *ELDER* and *OLDER* are alternative words with the same meaning. However, in common usage *elder* or *eldest* refer only to people, while *older* and *oldest* can refer to anything, people included. Generally, too, one would say "the elder of two children" but "the eldest of three."

Elderly   Here we run into a problem similar to that we encounter with youth. Be careful who you designate as ELDERLY. Most newswriters are fairly young people and tend to look upon anyone over 50 as elderly. Most people around 50 don't think of themselves as elderly, and are offended when someone else does. I think *elderly* may be safe in referring to someone more than 70. However, I'm around 50—or so.

Elicit/Illicit   *ELICIT* means to draw out, to find from someone —as the legal process attempts to elicit the truth. *ILLICIT* in most common use means illegal, unlawful or antisocial behavior.

Elude   *See* **Allude**.

Embargo   *See* **Wire Services**.

Emigrate/Immigrate   One *EMIGRATES* from a country and *IMMIGRATES* to another country. One leaving is an *emigrant* while one entering is an *immigrant*.

Eminent/Imminent   *EMINENT* means outstanding, prominent. *IMMINENT* means impending, soon to come, often with the connotation of a threat.

Empty/Vacant   The distinction here is fine and possibly non-existent. I believe usage has it that an *EMPTY* house is one with no people in it and a *VACANT* house is one with nothing in it. But, usage experts say "no." An empty bottle or house has nothing in it, while vacant carries the idea of a temporary condition—the folks away from home will soon return. Take your pick.

Engine/Motor   The two words are frequently used inter-changeably, but there are distinctions. A *MOTOR* uses an outside source of power, such as an electric motor, while an *ENGINE* generates its own power by consuming fuel. Another distinction is that a *motor* is generally station-ary, while an *engine* is used to move something about. That's not hard and fast, of course—we immediately encounter the stationary steam engine, and, after all, the motor vehicle. Let common usage determine which you choose.

Enigma/Puzzle/Riddle   An *ENIGMA* is a certain kind of *PUZZLE*. It is one that is stated in such a way as to be intentionally obscure—like a *RIDDLE*. It can also be a mysterious event. Enigma is not a good broadcast word—puzzle will usually do just fine.

Enormity   ENORMITY is not the same as enormousness. *Enormity* refers to a monstrous offense against decency or order.

En Route   Pronounced "ON ROOT." Why not write it *on route*?

Ensure/Insure   Some dictionaries say these two words, along with *assure* and *secure*, are synonymous, but I like the distinction between them. *ENSURE* means to make cer-tain, to make safe. *INSURE* refers to obtaining insurance, and in current usage, unless you are talking about the insurance business, use ensure.

Enthused/Enthusiastic *ENTHUSED* does not mean *ENTHUSIASTIC.* You cannot become enthused. It is a verb. You can certainly enthuse over something, but that usage is awkward and seldom used by serious writers and certainly not broadcast writers.

Enthusiasm Take care with the pronunciation. It is ehn-THOOZ-ee-AZ-um. It is often mispronounced as ehn-THOOZ-ee-IHZ-um.

Envelop/Envelope There is a pronunciation problem with these two closely related and common words. *ENVELOP* is pronounced ehn-VEL-up. *ENVELOPE* is pronounced EN-vuh-lohp.

Epidemic An *EPIDEMIC* is a rapidly-spreading disease and must be declared by competent medical authority—such as a local health director. Just because a lot of people have it doesn't make it an epidemic. It is considered a "scare" word in some circumstances and should be used with great care.

Epitome *See* **Acme.**

Epizootic There are times when for the sake of precision we have to use technical terms—and this is a perfect example. *EPIZOOTIC* refers to a disease or condition that is wide-spread among a certain group of animals, and *epidemic* may be a more familiar substitute, but we generally think of epidemics occurring among humans. The word came in handy a few seasons ago when several million turkeys and chickens became affected by avian flu in the Shenandoah Valley—a major poultry producing area. When we used the word, we briefly explained what it meant. It is pronounced ep-uh-zuh-WAHT-ik.

Erstwhile *ERSTWHILE* means former, once-upon-a-time. The erstwhile mayor is the one who did not win reelection. Its a pompous word—not recommended for broadcast news.

Escapee/Fugitive Here's one that no amount of prattling on my part will ever change, but did you ever stop to think that the person who escapes from prison is the escapor, while the jailor is the *ESCAPEE?* In any case, avoid it—use *FUGITIVE.*

Espresso   Note spelling. The strong steam-brewed coffee of Italian origin is *ESPRESSO*. It is NOT expresso.

Ethics/Morals   Books have been written on this one. For our purposes we'll simplify. *ETHICS* is the study of the ways we reach *MORAL* decisions. They are not synonymous. *Ethics* is always expressed as a plural, but treated as a singular—"ethics is."

Everybody/Everyone   Use "EVERYONE."

Excessive/Extensive   I recently heard it reported that the damage from a flood was EXCESSIVE. That may be true, but what the reporter meant to say was EXTENSIVE. *Excessive* means more than necessary. We speak of police sometimes using excessive force when they seem to overdo the physical action needed in an arrest. *Extensive* means over a wide area and, in common usage, to a severe degree.

Excuse   *See* **Alibi**.

Exotic   *EXOTIC* means coming from another country, foreign. It also has a secondary meaning of mysterious. The euphemism for "stripper" is "exotic dancer" which, like so many euphemisms, misses the mark completely.

Facade   A false front, of a building or a person. Pronounced fuh-SAWD.

Facility   A terribly overused word. *FACILITY* has to do with making things easier or more comfortable. Public toilets are correctly, although somewhat euphemistically, called facilities. A secondary meaning is something that is built for a specific purpose. A stadium is a sports facility, because that's what sportswriters call them.

Factor   Overused by lazy writers who want to say ingredient or component. *FACTOR* is a perfectly good word in those senses, but I hear it too often. *Factor* also means agent —one acting in behalf of another. *Factor* is a favorite word with writers who feel a need to puff up their copy. Anytime you are tempted to use *factor* look at your sentence carefully to see whether you can do without it.

Faint/Feint   Both pronounced FAYNT, but with vastly different meanings. *FAINT* can mean to lose consciousness, but we most often use the word to mean indistinct, difficult to see or hear. *FEINT* is a defensive move—used by boxers among others—to cause an opponent to make a wrong more. It can also mean any maneuver, physical or otherwise, to distract an opponent's attention.

Famous/Infamous/Notorious   *FAMOUS* means well-known or much talked about. *INFAMOUS* (pronounced IN-fuh-muss) means having a detestable reputation, known to be a truly awful person or thing. *NOTORIOUS* applies to people or things and means well-known for a particular trait or characteristic. It has a generally unsavory connotation.

Farther/Further   Many experts on usage are about to give up on the distinction, saying *FARTHER* is winning out. I think the distinction is worth preserving. *Farther* has to do with space or distance, while *FURTHER* can mean moreover or going beyond—as "further education." Please do not use the phrase "all the farther (or further)." That is unrecognizable as English.

Faze/Phase   Webster's gives *PHASE* as a variant spelling of *FAZE*. For our purposes, let's keep them apart because their meanings are so totally different. *Faze* means to worry, disconcert, bother, and is usually used in a negative sense: "He was unfazed by the weather." *PHASE* refers to a stage of development, a subdivision of time, place or completion.

February/Library   Note spellings and the fact that both have two "Rs" which are pronounced. It's FEB-roo-airy and LY-brair-ee.

Feel/Think   The old saw has it: You *FEEL* with your fingers and *THINK* with your head. How come people still write feel when they mean think or believe? Of course, it's possible to feel sad or ill, but one does not feel an idea. Come to think of it, feel seems to be pulling ahead as the word of choice for sloppy writers when they want think.

Felony/Misdemeanor   A *FELONY* is a serious crime for which a jail term can be handed down. A *MISDEMEANOR* is a less serious offense and usually does not carry a long jail term. However, recently judges have been jailing people convicted of drunken driving, which normally is considered a misdemeanor.

Fever/Temperature   Everyone has a *TEMPERATURE* and if all is well it will be about 98.6 F. If it is elevated we are said to have a *FEVER*. It is colloquial at best to say "I have a temperature." Of course you do.

Fewer/Less   *FEWER* refers to number while *LESS* refers to quantity. The illiterate commercial that tells you a certain beer is less filling (correct) because is has less calories (wrong) is an abomination. The language in those commercials may be a cynical attempt to reach to the "common man"—the beer drinkers. There is another commercial—this for light wine, in which the same phrase is used only slightly altered: "Less filling because it has fewer calories." Correct all the way. It gives you an idea of what sort of stereotypes are current on Madison Avenue.

Fiance/Fiancee   Both are pronounced fee-awn-SAY, and their meanings are identical—except for gender. The male of the couple engaged to be married is the *FIANCE*, while the female is the *FIANCEE*.

Figurative/Literal   If you use *LITERALLY* you'd better mean it. To write "The woman was so embarrassed, she literally died" means the lady is really dead. *FIGURATIVELY* has a metaphoric sense—where one thing is made to stand for another. In the example above, "The woman was so embarrassed she figuratively died" is correct, but silly.

Filipino/Philippines   Note spellings. A *FILIPINO* is a native of the *PHILIPPINE ISLANDS*.

Fin/Finn   A *FIN* can be an apendage on a fish or old slang for a five-dollar bill. A *FINN* is a native of Finland.

Firm   Not all businesses are FIRMS, but you wouldn't know it listening to broadcast news (or reading newspapers, for that matter), where everything becomes a firm. A *firm* is a business involving a partnership of two or more members. Therefore, a trucking business owned by one man is not a firm. Neither is the city-owned bus company.

Firmament   A quaint old word often misused. *FIRMAMENT* has nothing to do with firmness. In fact, it's about as far from that as you can get. It means the sky, the "Heavenly Arch."

First Annual   An impossibility. If it's the *FIRST* it cannot be *ANNUAL*—not yet, anyway. The phrase is full of hope but not good sense.

Firstly/Secondly/Thusly, Etc   Don't use them in broadcast copy.

First such...of its Kind   If it's the *FIRST SUCH* then *OF ITS KIND* is redundant—or certainly wordy. There are other similar constructions. Watch for them.

Flagrant   *See* **Blatant**.

Flammable/Inflammable   Isn't our language wonderful? These both mean the same thing, and there are many other similar seeming contradictions—words that begin with what we normally think of as a negative, but turn out not to be at all. *FLAMMABLE* and *INFLAMMABLE* both mean capable of burning. For broadcast use *flammable*.

Flash   *See* **Wire Services**.

Flash-in-the-Pan   I recently saw this phrased as "Splash in the pan." That doesn't make any sense. The reference is to what would occasionally happen with flint-lock weapons, when the flint spark would ignite the priming powder in the pan, but would fail to fire the gun—creating a "flash in the pan" but without result, a misfire.

Flaunt/Flout   Often confused; *FLAUNT* means to make a showy display, usually in a vulgar manner. *FLOUT* means to defy authority in a contemptuous manner, to mock.

Flautist/Flutist   For some reason we have two words for one who plays the flute. *FLAUTIST* is considered the "correct" one by serious musicians and others. *FLUTIST* is probably better understood by other folks.

Flew/Flied   Only in baseball is *FLIED* the accepted past tense of fly. "He flied out," for some reason, is okay on a ball diamond, except for the player who did it.

Flotsam/Jetsam   These terms were once limited to applying to ship wrecks. The *FLOTSAM* was the floating wreckage and the *JETSAM* certain cargo or other things tossed overboard in an attempt to save the ship, and which sinks or is beached. Today, they are used to describe almost anything floating or drifting about as if on water. We speak of "street people" as being the "flotsam and jetsam" of society.

Flounder/Founder   *FLOUNDER*, in addition to being a tasty flat fish, means to thrash around, to be out of control. *FOUNDER* is usually used in reference to ship sinkings. Its primary meaning is to fill with water and sink. Note that the idea of sinking is built in. It is redundant to say "The ship foundered and sank." Today we speak of businesses foundering. That's certainly apt.

Flu   *FLU* is an informal way of saying *influenza*, and that's not the sniffles. Influenza is a serious disease. Do not report that someone missed a meeting, for example, because of a "touch of the flu." There is no such thing as a touch of influenza. It is not a common cold.

Fluorescent   Mostly, look at the spelling.

Forbade   The past of *FORBID*. It is preferably pronounced for-BAD.

Foreign Words   Many very useful and colorful foreign words and phrases have found their way into daily speech. You should not avoid using them, as long as they are generally familiar. Be careful with the pronunciations, though— many such words have retained at least some of the foreign accenting, such as pizza (PEET-zuh) and espresso (not EX-press-oh). See also *ZUCCHINI*.

Forego/Forgo   Both spellings are considered correct. *FOREGO* means to pass up, to let go by, to abstain. It does not mean to go before, although Webster okays that sense.

Forging/Uttering   This will come up in forged check stories as well as others. *FORGING* is the actual writing of a check or other document with intent to defraud. *UTTERING* is the attempt to cash the check or exercise a forged document. The charge is usually expressed with both terms: "forging and uttering."

Former/Latter   Neither term should be used in broadcast copy to refer to something already stated. It's all right to identify someone as a "former Senator," but not to name two persons in paragraph one, then refer to them as the

FORMER or LATTER in paragraph two. The listener doesn't have time to figure it out. *Former* and *latter*, by the way, are used only when you are dealing with two persons or things. When more than two are involved, use *first* and *last*.

Formidable   Pronounced FOR-mid-ah-bul.

Fortuitous   A FORTUITOUS event is not necessarily a good thing. *Fortuitous* does not imply good fortune, only accident or fate—occurring by chance.

Forward   *See* **Afterward**.

Fracas   Pronounced FRAY-kus. It means a minor but physical encounter and can involve two or more individuals. Be careful not to write yourself an unintended double entendre—"The woman was shot in the fracas." It's a good old word, but has something of a slangy sound. It's fine describing a brawl.

Fractious   A terrible word for broadcast. It means to cause trouble by disobedience or unpredictable behavior.

Frankenstein   *FRANKENSTEIN* was the doctor, not the monster. If you ever have cause to use this to describe something that got out of hand, call it "a Frankenstein's monster."

Fugitive   *See* **Escapee**.

-Fuls   Most authorities now tell us the plural of spoonful is spoonfuls. Other "-FULS" are treated similarly. Spoonsful, which makes more literal and logical sense, is also acceptable. Oh well.

Fundamental   *See* **Basic**.

Funeral Service   A redundancy. A *FUNERAL* is a *SERVICE*.

Funny/Peculiar   Don't use *FUNNY* when you mean *PECULIAR* or strange.

Fusillade/Fuselage   A *FUSILLADE* (pronounced FYOO-sih-laud) is a hail of something, often bullets. A firing squad creates a fusillade. A *FUSELAGE* is the body of an airplane.

Gaff/Gaffe   *GAFF* has numerous meanings, most having to do

with a spear or pole used for some specific purposes—
such as gaffing fish or raising a sail. A *GAFFE* (still pronounced GAFF) is a social blunder.

Gage/Gauge   We sometimes see GAGE used where GAUGE is
needed. A *gage* is the cap or glove that's thrown on the
ground to invite an opponent to fight. A *gauge* is usually a
measuring device. The verb form *to gauge* refers to
measuring or judging.

Gamut/Gantlet/Gauntlet   The correct phrase, although a
cliché, is to "run the GANTLET." It is frequently and
incorrectly phrased as "run the GAUNTLET." A *gauntlet*
is a long glove such as a welder or horseman might wear. a
gantlet is formed by two rows of people between which
someone runs while being beaten with sticks. Another
thing we seem to run a lot is a GAMUT. That means to
run the whole range of something. It originated as a
musical term—to run the *gamut* meant to run the whole
musical scale from one extreme to the other.

Gauge   *See* **Caliber**.

Gender/Sex   Both words refer to the difference between males
and females and *GENDER* also refers to certain linguistic
formations. In broadcast copy, *sex* is preferred, as it is
almost anywhere.

Generic/Genetic   These words are related, both stemming from
genus. Something that is *GENERIC* is characteristic of
the whole genus. Thus, it has been extended to include
such things as generic drugs, bread, and cigarettes—sold
without brand names. *GENETIC* refers to genes and to
origins and can be applied to both animate and inanimate
things.

Genteel/Gentile   A *GENTEEL* person is one who is polite,
stylish. It also means living in an elegant manner. A
GENTILE is a non-Jewish person, usually a Christian.

Genuine   Pronounce it JEN-yoo-win.

Girl Friend   *See* **Boy Friend**.

Girl/Woman   *See* **Boy**.

Glamour   This is among the few words in American English to
retain the British "OUR" ending.

Glance/Glimpse The error here is to use GLANCE for GLIMPSE. A *glance* is the physical act of *glimpsing*. You get a *glimpse* of something when you *glance* at it. The *glance* is the quick sidelong look, the quick sight you get is the *glimpse*. Got it? Don't work too hard at it, in common use the words are almost interchangable.

Golf/Gulf Pronunciation problems with these words. The game is pronounced "GAWLF;" the abyss or body of water is pronounced "GUHLF."

Gorilla/Guerrilla Another pronunciation problem. The great ape is pronounced "guh-RILL-uh." The irregular soldier is pronounced "gehr-RILL-uh," in American English. It's a Spanish word meaning, literally, *small war*.

Got/Gotten These are ugly sounding words when spoken—avoid them in broadcast copy. Often *got* is used unnecessarily. Pennsylvanians are stuck with auto license tags that read "You've got a friend in Pennsylvania." Leave out the got and you still have: "You have a friend in Pennsylvania," which says exactly the same thing in a much nicer way. I have seen Pennsylvania tags with the got taped over; that's gratifying.

Gourmand/Gourmet A *GOURMAND* is a person who likes to eat—usually a lot. A *GOURMET* (pronounced goor-MAY) is a person who knows a lot about and appreciates good food, but is not necessarily a heavy eater. *Gourmet*, although widely used as an adjective is recognized only as a noun. It is technically incorrect to speak of "gourmet food."

Graduate You are *GRADUATED from* a high school or an institution of higher learning. It is an action taken by the school. Think about the word—it has to do with making the grade. It is nonstandard to say "He graduated from..." It is correct to say "He was graduated from..." Never say "He graduated college."

Granada/Grenada *GRANADA* is a city in Spain and is pronounced gruh-NAWD-uh. *GRENADA* is an island in the West Indies and is pronounced greh-NAYD-uh. Note the different spellings.

Graffiti/Graffito Note spellings—two Fs, one T. *GRAFFITI* is the plural.

Gratuitous   *GRATUITOUS* means unearned or unnecessary. It has nothing to do with graciousness and is only distantly related to gratitude when used in the sense of something that is given without cost to the recipient. We speak of gratuitous violence (unnecessary) in television action programs.

Grill/Grille   This is a difference without much of a distinction. A *GRILL* usually has to do with cooking food or the place that serves grilled food. A *GRILLE* is a barred structure forming a gate or screen. It's also the front of an automobile above the bumper. *Grill* can be used for either. Don't worry about it too much.

Grip/Grippe   *Grip* means to hold firmly and in television you will find a person who assists a photographer known as the "key grip." His or her job is to set up or hold lights, string microphone cables, and generally be around to lug equipment. *GRIPPE* is a viral disease resembling influenza, still pronounced GRIP.

Grisly/Gristly/Grizzly   A bloody scene, such as a bad highway crash, can be described as *GRISLY*. A tough piece of cartilage in meat is said to be *GRISTLY* and is pronounced GRIZ-uh-lee. The bear is the *GRIZZLY*.

Guadeloupe/Guadalupe   *GUADELOUPE* is two islands in the French West Indies. *GUADALUPE* is an island owned by Mexico off the coast of southern California, among other things and places. Both are pronounced gwahd-ehl-OOP.

Guardrail/Guiderail   There may be such things as GUIDE-RAILS, but they are not found beside highways—those are GUARDRAILS.

Guest Host   This apparently contradictory phrase is well-understood whenever Johnny Carson goes on vacation. Watch for "oxymorons," they will creep in. An oxymoron is a figure of speech which is deliberately contradictory. It comes from the Greek meaning sharply foolish. Webster gives "cruel kindness" as another example.

Guide/Guy Wires   A frequent error. The cables that support towers, bridges and so on, are *GUY WIRES* not GUIDE wires.

Gun/Weapon   *See* **Automatic**.

Gutted   It's slangy and crude, but accepted, to say fire GUTTED the inside of a building. However, we cannot extend that usage to say fire gutted 35 acres of woods.

Gynecology   A branch of medicine relating to the health of women, usually associated with the reproductive organs. It is pronounced GYN-eh-CAWL-eh-jee, with a hard "G". Many other words beginning with "gy" are pronounced with a soft "G", such as *gyroscope, gyration, gypsom.*

Habit/Practice   Don't say HABIT when you mean PRACTICE. *Habit* implies fixation or compulsion, not simply doing something in a predictable way. For instance, it is misleading to say "He's in the habit of driving to work along Main Street." A habitual act occurs without planning.

Habitable/Inhabitable/Uninhabitable   Here we hit another of those weird words. *HABITABLE* and *INHABITABLE*— both mean the same thing: capable of being lived in. *UNINHABITABLE* means you wouldn't want to live there.

Hail/Hale   *HAIL* is the frozen precipitation, the greeting, and the salutation as in "all hail the chief." *HALE* means healthy and also means to haul someone into court.

Half Mast/Half Staff   Flags on land are flown at *HALF STAFF*. It is, after all, a flag staff. At sea, flags are most often flown from a mast, so there they are said to fly at *HALF MAST*.

Halley's Comet   As this is written HALLEY'S COMET has swung around the Sun and is returning to deep space. It will be the subject of much writing and talking for months—perhaps years—to come. What you need to know is this: it rhymes with "Valley."

Hallowe'en   Note the spelling. It is a contraction of All Hallows' Evening, the night before All Hallow's Day. The pronunciation is often HAWL-oh-een. It is better HAL-ow-een. Webster accepts the spelling "halloween," without the apostrophe. Why not?

Handkerchief   Pronounced HAND-ker-chiff. Be careful not to drop the "d" so it comes out "hanker-chiff."

Hangar/Hanger   Aircraft are stored and repaired in a HANGAR. The most common use of HANGER is to refer to clothes hangers—but it has a number of other uses as well.

Hanged/Hung   A condemned person is said to have been HANGED, while a picture is HUNG on the wall.

Happen/Occur/Transpire   Accidents don't HAPPEN, they occur. *Occur* is the preferred verb when the action is spontaneous or accidental. The words are very similar in meaning, but occur is preferred when referring to the unexpected. *TRANSPIRE* is a pompous word for to take place, and is usually used incorrectly. It means, literally, to exhale across. It also has a meaning of coming to light, of exposing, to become known. It does not mean to *happen* or *occur*.

Harass   Often misspelled and mispronounced. It is spelled as you see it here, and its preferred pronunciation is heh-RASS.

Harbor/Port   A *HARBOR* is any safe haven on a coast line where a ship can enter to be protected from the open sea. A *PORT* is usually located in a harbor and is the complex of dock, wharfs, and piers against which ships may moor. The idea of port extends to the city itself.

Healthful/Healthy   A distinction is normally drawn between HEALTHFUL and HEALTHY. *Healthful* is taken to mean promoting or contributing to health. We speak of healthful foods. *Healthy* is a state of being, free of disease and functioning properly.

Heart Attack   *See* **Coronary.**

Height   Note spelling. It is not heighth, as many people seem to believe, influenced, no doubt, by width and depth.

Heinous   Pronounced HAY-nuss. It means shocking, grossly evil.

Helicopter   Pronounced HELL-ih-copter.

Heroin/Heroine   These words are identically pronounced "HAIR-oh-win." Be careful not to refer to the brave lady as a "heroin."

Hoar/Whore   *HOAR* is frost. An old person with white hair is said to be *hoary-haired*. We all know what a WHORE is. I would urge you to use either word with great caution.

Hoard/Horde   To *HOARD* is to gather up large quantities of food or other materials against possible future shortages. During World War II when rationing was imposed, hoarding was a serious offense. The word carries with it the implication of greed. *Hoard* is also used as a noun as in "a hoard of gold." A *HORDE* is a large number of people; the sense of being unorganized is built in.

Hoi Polloi   Many people seem to think the HOI POLLOI are the fancy folks, the elite. Not so. The *hoi polloi* are the common folks—the masses. Pronounced HOY puh-LOY.

Holocaust   Originally *HOLOCAUST* referred to sacrifice by fire, then destruction or any big fire. It has come to mean the destruction of European Jews by the Nazis, and perhaps has been preempted from other uses. That's what happens to a dynamic language. It's too bad, perhaps, but such words as *gay* and *queer* have also been lost in their original senses.

Home/House   A HOUSE is not a HOME. A *house* is a structure intended to be lived in but which may or may not be occupied. A *home* is any place a person or group of persons lives: a house, apartment, or tent.

Homicide/Manslaughter/Murder   To cause the death of any human being by whatever means is a *HOMICIDE* (note spelling). *MANSLAUGHTER* is the unlawful killing of another person without malice or premeditation. A *MURDER* is the unlawful, willful, malicious or predmeditated killing of another human being. There are, in most states, several "degrees" of murder.

Hopefully   Do not use *HOPEFULLY* as an adverb in the sense of "it is to be hoped" at the beginning of a sentence: "Hopefully, the car will arrive on time." That means the car is full of hope. There's a deep urge in all of us to use hopefully and "thankfully" that way; don't.

...To A Hospital   Use "...To A HOSPITAL" rather than "to the hospital," or name the specific hospital to which someone is taken. A word of caution: in most localities in which there is more than one hospital, one will develop into the "emergency" hospital. Logically, that is the place where most accident victims and other emergency cases will die. If you name the hospital each time, it will soon become known to the public as a pest house—the place you go to die; just a thought.

Hot Cup Of. . .   Some authorities are saying it is sheer sophistry to insist that it's not a HOT CUP OF something, but a "cup of hot" something. But, I still like the precision. It is not the cup that is hot, but rather, what is in it.

Hot Water Heater   Same thing here. It is not a *HOT WATER HEATER*, but a *water heater.*

Hudson's Bay   The huge body of water north of Canada is *HUDSON'S BAY*, not Hudson Bay.

Humongous   The word is a combination of huge and tremendous. It is slang. Don't use it.

Hurdle/Hurtle   These words have similar sound and meaning and are often confused. *HURDLE* means to leap over an obstacle. *HURTLE* means to plunge rapidly as in "the rocket hurtled through space." Careful pronunciation is needed.

Hurricane   *See* **Cyclone.**

Hyper/Hypo   *HYPER* as a prefix means above, in excess; as an adjective it means overexcitable. *HYPO* is the opposite, it means below, less than normal. We speak of hypothermia when the body temperature is severely below normal and hypertension when the blood pressure is seriously elevated.

If/Whether   WHETHER has a built-in sense of "or not," implying alternative choices. If that is the sense of your idea, then use *whether.* Otherwise, use IF. Most often, "or not" is not needed with whether. Test your sentence to see whether you can leave out the "or not."

Ilk   It's not what you think, if you think it means something like "people he associates with." Your *ILK* are those of your family—with the same name. It's an old Scottish word, heard infrequently and mostly pejoratively these days. "MacDonald and his ilk."

Ill/Sick   Prefer ILL most of the time. But, "the scene sickened even the hardened police," is much stronger than "The scene made even the hardened police ill."

Illicit   *See* **Elicit.**

Illusion   *See* **Allusion.**

Immature/Premature   *IMMATURE* means unfinished, not fully grown or developed. *PREMATURE* means before it's time, unexpectedly early. In referring to premature babies, there are two measures: born before the full gestation period is complete, or with lower than normal birth weight, regardless of the gestation period.

Immigrate   *See* **Emigrate.**

Imminent   *See* **Eminent.**

Immolate   We became familiar with this word during the Viet Nam war when Bhuddist monks were said to have committed self-IMMOLATION when they burned themselves to death publicly. That is a correct use of the word, but many people now think immolation necessarily involves burning. An *immolation* is a sacrifice, sometimes involving killing one's self or someone else, but the word can also be used symbolically, and immolation does not necessarily involve fire.

Immoral   *See* **Amoral.**

Impeach   When a public official is charged with official misconduct he or she is said to have been IMPEACHED. Note that an *impeachment* involves ONLY the bringing of charges. It is like an indictment. Under the U.S. Constitution, the House of Representatives, after hearings, can impeach a sitting President. But, the actual trial is conducted by the Senate. The President can be found either guilty or innocent of the impeachment.

Imply/Infer   The easiest way to handle this confusion is to remember that the speaker *IMPLIES* and the listener *INFERS*. It's not always oral communication, of course.

Impotent/Imprudent/Impudent   The pronunication of IMPO-TENT is IM-puht-unt. Therefore, it is often confused with IMPUDENT which is often confused with IMPRU-DENT. *Impotent* means powerless, helpless, weak.

Impudent means cocky, bold, without regard for others, disrespectful. *IMPRUDENT* means lacking caution, without regard for consequences.

Incipient/Insipid Here are a pair of almost look-and-sound alikes that have very different meanings. *INCIPIENT* means something that is about to come into being. A person about to be graduated from a teacher's college, for example, is an incipient teacher. *INSIPID*, on the other hand, means dull, lacking in taste. The word can be applied to people or things, such as soup.

Incorporated *See* **Corporation.**

Indecision *See* **Ambivalence.**

Indict An INDICTMENT (pronounced in-DIYT-munt) is carried out by a Grand Jury. An *indictment* is a statement that a crime has been committed and there is sufficient evidence to bring the accused to trial. It is not a finding of guilt or innocence. The finding of a Grand Jury to bring the accused to trial is called a "true bill." If there is not an indictment the finding is called "no true bill."

Indifferent *See* **Diffident.**

Infamous *See* **Famous.**

Infant *See* **Baby.**

Infectious *See* **Contagious.**

Inflammable *See* **Flammable.**

Informant/Informer Both have the meaning of "one who informs." However *INFORMER* is the word of choice when speaking of someone who "squeals." "The police informer."

Inhabitable *See* **Habitable.**

Inhuman/Inhumane These mean about the same thing, but it seems to me that *INHUMAN* refers to actions affecting people, while *INHUMANE* relates to animals. They both mean to be cruel and insensitive to the feelings, comfort or safety of others.

Injured *See* **Damaged.**

Inmate *See* **Convict.**

Innocent/Not Guilty   There is a difference between INNO-CENT and NOT GUILTY. The verdict of a court will be "not guilty," it will not be "innocent," because *innocence* is a state of being, not an official finding. In broad-casting we do better to say a person was "acquitted" rather than found "not guilty," because of the possibility of being misunderstood.

Inoculate   Note the spelling—just one N.

Inquiry/Question   *INQUIRY* has the sense of being more than just asking a QUESTION. An *inquiry* is the seeking of truth or facts and the examination of that information. One would ask questions while conducting an inquiry.

Inside/Outside   Do not use with "...of" unless *INSIDE* or *OUTSIDE* is used as a noun. "The inside of the boiler was damaged" is correct. But, "He tossed the body inside of the boiler" is not.

Insidious/invidious   Both are unpleasant. *INSIDIOUS* means cunning, deceitful, creeping slowly with, most likely, a hidden effect. *INVIDIOUS* means defamatory, likely to cause discontent, jealous.

In Spite of   *See* **Despite.**

Instantaneously/Instantly   INSTANTANEOUSLY is what we usually want when we say INSTANTLY. *Instantaneously* means with no perceptible lapse of time. *Instantly* means without delay, at once, with urgency.

Insure   *See* **Ensure.**

Intended/Intentional   What is *INTENDED* is what is meant by or expected from some speech or action. *INTENTIONAL* means deliberately—on purpose.

Inter/Intra   *INTER* as a prefix means among or between, as in "inter-national" or "inter-relation." *INTRA* means with-in, inside as in "intravenous injection" or "intramural."

Inundated   *INUNDATED* means flooded. To write: "inundated by flood waters" is a redundancy.

Irregardless   IRREGARDLESS of how many times you've seen this word—it is not a word. The word wanted is *regardless*.

Irrevocable Pronounced eer/REV-uh-kuh-bul. Study the "IR-" words in a good dictionary. Pronunciation of many is tricky.

Isle of Wight In the United States probably the only people who need to worry about this are those in Virginia where there is an Isle of Wight County and a town of the same name. The original is an island in the English Channel. The thing to note here is the spelling and pronunciation—it is "WIGHT"—not "white."

Israeli/Israelite A modern native of the Republic of Israel is an *ISRAELI*. A member of one of the 10 Hebrew tribes of ancient times is called an *ISRAELITE*.

Its/It's *ITS* is the possessive and is formed without an apostrophe. *IT'S* is the contraction of "it is." This is confusing, because most possessives are formed with an apostrophe as in "Murphy's Law."

Jail/Prison/Penitentiary Some dictionaries claim JAIL and PRISON are synonymous, but usage dictates a distinction. A *jail* is a local lockup where newly-arrested persons are held pending trial, or where short-term prisoners are housed (see *CONVICT*). A *PRISON* is a state or federal penal institution where convicted prisoners are incarcerated. A *PENITENTIARY* is the same as a prison and refers to a major big house. One would not refer to the city prison or the state jail.

Jerry/Jury Something done for temporary or emergency purposes is said to be "JURY rigged," such as a spar erected on a ship in place of a broken mast. Something that is hastily or sloppily done is said to be "JERRY built." It is a term of contempt. Some authorities believe it stems from World War II when German troops were referred to as "Jerries." Webster says it's much older.

Jetsam *See* **Flotsam.**

Join Together A redundancy.

Judge/Jurist/Juror We all know what a JUDGE is, but we get confused over JURIST. A *jurist* is not a member of a jury. A *jurist* is a person skilled in the law. He or she might be a judge or an attorney, or not. A JUROR is a member of a Jury.

Judgment Note spelling—not judgement. That's correct in Britain, however. A recent U.S. President, I'm sure, spelled it wrong because he pronounced it as three syllables: judge-uh-ment.

Judicial/Judicious *JUDICIAL* has to do with the process of judging, the administration of justice. Court proceedings are said to be judicial actions. *JUDICIOUS* refers to the exercise of sound judgment, not necessarily in connection with court actions. Characterized by reasoning and sound logic.

Juggler/Jugular A *JUGGLER* is a person who can keep several objects in the air seemingly at the same time. It is used literally to describe someone putting on a show, and figuratively to describe a busy person with many projects underway at once. The *JUGULAR* is a large vein in the neck which, when severed, allows a person (or animal) to bleed to death rapidly. To say a person is "going for the 'jugular'," means he or she is out to literally or figuratively kill an opponent. Note it is a three-syllable word: JUHG-yoo-luhr.

Junction/Juncture A *JUNCTION* is a place of meeting, in its most common use. A railroad *junction* is a point where two or more rail lines come together. A *JUNCTURE* is most often used to indicate a point in time, but it also can mean a coming together, a seam.

Junta A *JUNTA* is a group of people, usually military, who are placed in control of a government following a coup (see **Coup d'etat**). It is a Spanish word, therefore pronounced HOON-tah or HUN-tah.

Karat *See* **Carat**.

Ketchup *See* **Catsup**.

Kidnaped This is the preferred spelling for print journalists, but for broadcast use KIDNAPPED. The "PP" prevents mispronunciation.

Kill *See* **Wire Services**.

Killed After   This is one we see with frightening regularity. The man was KILLED AFTER his car struck the tree. Did they run over him with the ambulance? He may have "died after" the wreck, but he was not "killed after" the crash.

Kilo   Pronounced KEE-loh. It is an abbreviation of kilogram, usually. A *KILO* is one-thousand grams or approximately two-and-a-half pounds.

Kilometer   Pronounced kuh-LAWM-jht-ur. It is the metric system's equivalent of the mile and is one-thousand meters or approximately six-tenths of a U.S. mile.

Knot   One nautical mile. It is a measure of speed, not of distance. The sense of time is built-in. A ship is said to be making 10 knots, not 10 knots-an-hour. A nautical mile is approximately one-and-one-tenth statute miles.

Kudos   Always written as if plural. It refers to praise offered following an achievement. Mostly limited to public performances. The audience heaped KUDOS on the actor.

Lady/Woman   Don't use LADY when you are simply referring to a person of the female persuasion. *Lady* is a term of respect or honor.

Laid/Lain/Lay/Lie   *LAID* is the past participle of *LAY*, *LAIN* is the past participle of *LIE*. *LAY* has many meanings, but the most common usage would be the act of laying something down. *LIE* is a verb that does not take an object (an intransitive verb). "I will lie down." People have problems mostly with the past tense and past participle of these words. The past tense of *lie* is *lay*, and the past participle is *lain*. The past tense and participle of *lay* are both *laid*. Look to your dictionary for further discussion. The whole mess is admittedly confusing.

Laissez Faire   Pronounced le-say-FAYR. It means to let things find their own way, without government direction. It is a doctrine of certain economists.

Last/Latest   Both have the meaning of "most recent," but, *LAST* also means final. One's LATEST breath and one's *last* breath are very different things, indeed.

Lath/Lathe   A *LATH* is a thin strip of wood used primarily for the underlayment of wall and celling plaster. A *LATHE* (pronounced LAYTH) is a machine for turning and shaping wood.

Latinates   These are the many words in our language that derive from Latin roots. Their plurals often cause problems because in common usage the Latin rules have broken down. For example, we once had one *agendum*, but two *agenda*. Today, *agenda* is the accepted singular, and we rarely hear *agendum*. The common plural is *agendas*. Still clinging to life, but by an ever-thinning thread—is *datum* as the singular and *data* as the plural. Only the most pure of the purists still insist on *stadia*. And for broadcast use we would refer to *referendums* and *curriculums* even though academicians shudder. *Media* is plural. The only time you would refer to *mediums* is when there is more than one person conducting a séance. We are often called upon to use *criteria*. Always remember, it is plural. The singular is *criterion*. If the occasion ever arises that you feel compelled to use the plural of *syllabus*, you have a real problem. Both *syllabi* and *syllabusses* sound "sylly." If you have doubts, consult your friend Webster.

Latitude/Longitude   *LATITUDE* is a measure of distance North or South of the Equator. *LONGITUDE* is the distance East or West from Greenwich, England. Both are expressed in degrees, minutes, and seconds. *"Longitude"* is also expressed as time. One degree of latitude varies from approximately 69 miles at the Equator to approximately 70 miles at the poles. One degree of longitude varies from approximately 69-and-a-half miles at the Equator to zero at the poles.

Latter   *See* **Former.**

Lawyer   *See* **Attorney.**

Lease/Rent   A *LEASE* is a contract arranging to RENT something. You do not lease an apartment, you sign a lease to rent the apartment.

Leave/Let   LEAVE me alone and LET me alone do not mean the same thing. *Leave* means just that—go away and leave me here my myself. *Let* means stop bothering me.

Lectern   *See* **Dais.**

Legalese   The language of the law is filled with jargon, much of it based on Latin. Your job as a broadcast newswriter is to interpret, not to parrot. Do not inform Aunt Tillie that a fiduciary has been named, nor that a writ of certiorari is on file. She, and most other people, have no idea what you're talking about. Get a copy of a good legal dictionary for your newsroom, and use it.

Legible/Readable   In common use *LEGIBLE* and *READABLE* mean the same thing—capable of being read. Use *readable.*

Lend/Loan   Some authorities are saying that *LOAN* is becoming accepted as a verb. There is a nice distinction between loan and LEND that should be preserved...*lend* is the verb and *loan* is the noun. "Lend me your book." "I took out a loan." Kilpatrick suggests that *lend* applies to animate things as in "...lend me a hand," while *loan* applies to inanimate objects. I don't know where that came from. Many dictionaries and usage guides are accepting *loan* as a verb.

Less   *See* **Fewer.**

Liable/Libel   Easily and often confused. To be *LIABLE* is to be obligated or responsible for something, or less formally, to be likely to be exposed to something—a teacher is liable to catch students' colds. *LIBEL* is a form of defamation. If a journalist defames the subject of a news story he or she is liable to be sued for libel.

Libel/Slander   Both are forms of defamation. The difference lies in how widespread the defamation becomes. Defamation, when published, either in print or by broadcast, is *LIBEL.* Defamation that is unpublished, as in a conversation or in correspondence, is *SLANDER.* Both generally require that what is said is maliciously false and damaging to the subject's character and reputation. Libel law is complex and frequently changes. As a broadcaster, you will do well to keep up with it. See Appendix VII for a further discussion.

Library   *See* **February.**

Lighted/Lit   Either is considered an acceptable past tense of the verb to light. For broadcast, prefer *LIGHTED.*

Lightening/Lightning   LIGHTENING has three syllables—LYTen-ing. LIGHTNING has only two—LYT-ning. *Lighten-ing* has to do with making something less heavy or less dark. *Lightning* is the electrical accompaniment to a thunderstorm.

Like *See* **As If**.

Like/Such As Dictionaries accept the use of *LIKE* in the sense of *SUCH AS*. However, confusion can result, so let's use *such as*, even though it may sound a little more formal. Kilpatrick makes a strong case for the distinction. He says "...places like New York's Bellevue Hospital Center..." refers to other similar places, but excludes Bellevue. "...places such as New York's Bellevue Hospital Center..." includes Bellevue and other similar hospitals. He offers several other examples and a good discussion.

Lingerie It's pronounced lawn-zhu-RAY.

Litany/Liturgy Frequently confused. A LITANY can be part of a LITURGY. A *litany* is the ritual repetition of incantations or prayers. It has come to mean the detailing of any list, as in: "He reeled off a litany of wants and needs." *Liturgy* is a rite prescribed for public worship services specifically in Christian churches in observance of traditional form.

Literally *See* **Figuratively**.

Live *See* **Dwell**.

Livid Some authorities (see Kilpatick) are giving up on this one. Most people, for some reason, believe that *LIVID* means reddish. It does not. *Livid* means ashen, pale gray. When a person is said to be "livid with anger" he or she is so angry he or she has gone white, not red.

Loath/Loathe *LOATH* means a reluctance to do something, *LOATHE* refers to an intense dislike, hatred. The "TH" sounds differ. Loath gets a short sound as in Smith, Loathe gets a longer sound, as in with.

Love A score of nothing in tennis. It was recently reported in connection with baseball that "the score is three-love" in the sense that the score was tied at three each. That's plain wrong. What the sports writer wanted was "three-all."

Luxuriant/Luxuriate/Luxurious *LUXURIANT* refers to abundance, usually of plant growth. We speak of luxuriant fields of wheat. *LUXURIATE* in the common use means to live in luxury, in which case you would be living in LUXURIOUS surroundings.

Mad *See* **Angry.**

Magic/Miracle Take care in serious writing that MAGIC and MIRACLE are used in the proper context. There are very, very few "miracles" these days and "magic" is sleight of hand. A *miracle* would be something that happened beyond human comprehension, supernatural. The rescue of the victim of a near-drowning, for example, might have been difficult or spectacularly carried out, but it would not be called a miracle; almost a miracle, perhaps.

Majority/Plurality A *MAJORITY* is a number greater than half the total. A *PLURALITY* occurs when, for example, there are more than two candidates running for the same office. The one winning among three holds a plurality, not a majority, unless he or she alone polls more than half the total of all three. *Majority* applies only to things you can count. It is nonstandard to refer to a majority of your writing. It is not a synonym for "the major part, or "the largest portion."

Manslaughter *See* **Homicide.**

Mantel/Mantle Soundalikes that have quite different meanings. A *MANTEL* is the trimming around and shelf above a fireplace. A *MANTLE* is, among other things, a robe or shawl, a cloak. We also speak of the Earth's *mantle*, that portion of the interior between the crust and the core. A *mantle* is something that surrounds or covers. It is also used symbolically: "He assumed the mantle of office." That's pompous and not a good metaphor for broadcast. We often see the fireplace decoration referred to as a mantle, and that spelling may be emerging as acceptable.

Manual Labor/Physical Labor *MANUAL LABOR* has to do with working with one's hands. It is not necessarily strenuous work. *PHYSICAL LABOR* is generally considered to be hard work involving the whole body. Grinding lenses is manual labor, digging ditches is physical labor.

Margin/Score   A SCORE of 9-to-5 is not a MARGIN. In that example, the margin would be four. The *margin* is the difference between the two.

Marginal   Do not confuse MARGINAL with small. *Marginal* means, in one sense, near the lower limits of acceptability, just barely qualifying. That may be where the idea that marginal means small comes from. But it doesn't.

Marine/Nautical   The word *NAUTICAL* pertains specifically to ships or navigation. It is not standard to refer to "nautical life." What is meant is MARINE life. *Marine* refers to both ships and other aspects of the sea. It has been extended to refer to fresh water as well.

Marital/Martial/Marshal/Marshall   *MARITAL* (having to do with the state of being married) and *MARTIAL* (having to do with the military) need to be clearly marked in broadcast copy because they are so very easy to confuse. Sound-alikes MARSHAL and MARSHALL are also easily confused. *Marshal* is a military rank or someone who leads a public event such as a parade. *Marshall* is someone's name.

Mass/Service   A *MASS* is a *SERVICE* in certain churches. The services in those churches (usually Catholic) are always referred to as a mass. A mass, depending on the church and the type of mass it is, is said to be read, sung or celebrated, but never preached.

Masterful/Masterly   *MASTERFUL* implies dominance—a strong personality, imposing one's will on others. *MASTERLY* implies competence, doing something with the skill of a master. Neither implies maleness—and can be applied to either men or women.

Material/Materiel   *MATERIAL* has a number of meanings, most having to do with physical objects, such as cloth, paving materials and so on. *MATERIEL* is a much narrower term referring to supplies for a military operation. It is pronounced muh-TEER-ee-ELL.

Matinee   A *MATINEE* is a performance, so to say "matinee performance" is a redundancy. A *matinee* is, by definition, a daytime performance, usually in the afternoon.

May   *See* **Can.**

Mayonnaise   There are three syllables here--MAY-uh-NAYZ. It is not MAN-ayz or any such variant.

Meaningful   So overused as to be nauseating (See **Nauseated**).

Meanwhile   Be careful of using MEANWHILE as a transition to mean "at the same time." *Meanwhile* suggests an interval, an intervening period of time.

Media   If you learn nothing else here, learn this: *MEDIA* is plural! *Mediums* is not the proper plural of medium. See **Latinates**. It is "the television medium, but "the mass media."

Median/Medium   The grassy divider between two highways is called the *MEDIAN*, not the MEDIUM. Median strip is a redundancy. A concrete divider between two roadways is correctly called a median divider.

Medical Examiner   *See* **Coroner**.

Medication   *See* **Drugs**.

Medicine   *See* **Drugs**.

Melee   This is often mispronounced. It is correctly MAY-lay. It means a fight among several persons. It's probably better to call a fight a fight.

Memento   This error occurs too often to be a mere typo, although that's what it looks like. The word is *MEMENTO*, meaning something to remember me by, an object that stirs memory. Careless writers and speakers often use momento.

Memo   An acceptable abbreviation of "memorandum."

Memoranda/Memorandums   Take your pick for the plural of memorandum. Purists will stick with the Latinate, but those striving for conversational speech will use the English version. There are many words from the Latin that pose similar problems. Usage will eventually level them out. *See* **Latinates**.

Meretricious/Meritorious   Two look-alikes that have very different meanings. *MERETRICIOUS* means to exhibit attractions based on deceit or pretense, originally relating to a prostitute. *MERITORIOUS* means deserving of merit, worthy of reward.

Metal/Mettle   *METTLE* is most often used to suggest strength or stamina: "he proved his mettle." It also refers to temperament, strength of character. *METAL*, of course, refers to any metalic substance, such as iron or aluminum.

Meticulous   Not a compliment. A *METICULOUS* person is one who is fussily painstaking for fear of error or criticism.

Midair   There is no such place. Undoubtedly a headline word. Certainly planes may collide in flight, or in the air, but not in MIDAIR.

Minimize   *See* **Diminish**.

Minion   We frequently hear police referred to as MINIONS of the law—with the sense that *minion* means upholder or enforcer. Not so. *Minion* means either one who is admired or a subordinate—a follower, dependant. Yes, it is confusing, not to mention contradictory.

Minuscule   Note spelling. It comes from the same root as minor, not from the root of miniature. *MINUSCULE* does mean very small, however. Use miniature, if it fits. You certainly would not refer to "...a miniature amount," however.

Misdemeanor   *See* **Felony**.

Mishap   *See* **Accident**.

Monday, Etc...   When pronouncing the days of the week—fully pronounce "-DAY." It is MUN-day, not MUN-dee.

Mongoloid Idiot   Avoid this phrase. In the past it was accepted as a common adjective for a sufferer of mongolism or Down's Syndrome. It is now considered derogatory. Not all Down's victims are "idiots," although many are mentally retarded.

Monstrous   Yes, *MONSTROUS* means huge, but it also means grossly abnormal, horrifying. The sense is an act or thing that is deliberately or inherently evil—a monstrous lie.

Morals   *See* **Ethics**.

Morbid/Sordid   *MORBID* in common use can mean susceptible to gloom or depression. It also means gruesome. *SORDID* means either filthy or gross, vile.

More Than/Over   Picky editors will land on this one every time.

MORE THAN refers to quantity, *OVER* refers to a spatial relationship. Therefore, to say "Over one-million-dollars" will earn you a nasty look from Ed.

Mortgage Pronounced MOHR-gidj.

Motor *See* **Engine**.

Murder *See* **Homicide**.

Naked/Nude Both mean without clothing but for broadcast, use NUDE.

Naphtha See **Diphtheria**.

Nation *See* **Country**.

Nauseated/Nauseous You become NAUSEATED when you see something NAUSEOUS. You cannot feel nauseous. Please pay attention to this—it's a frighteningly common mistake.

Nautical *See* **Marine**.

Naval *NAVAL* pertains only to the navy. It is a term referring to the watery military only, not generally to ships.

Near Miss OOOPS. We hear this phrase in air traffic stories often—it is a nonsense phrase. Think about it. If it was nearly a miss, it was a hit! What happened was a near collision, not a "near miss."

New innovation A redundancy—an *INNOVATION* is new by definition.

News/Press Conference We broadcasters run very few presses. Let's refer to the occasions as NEWS conferences, rather than the more restrictive PRESS conferences. "The press" is used generically to refer to all journalists, of course. I wish there was another word.

New York *See* **State of**...

Nice A waffling adjective. Find a better one.

Nobody/None/No One They all mean NO ONE or NOT ONE. Use no one or not one. Note that they are all treated as a singular: "None is going."

Noisome/Noxious A common and quite understandable confusion surrounds NOISOME. It refers not to noise, but to smell. Something that smells offensive is said to be *noisome*. It is not necessarily poisonous, so don't confuse noisome with *NOXIOUS*, which is something that is harmful, but does not necessarily smell bad. Noisome is not a good broadcast word.

Normalcy/Normality   Both mean the state of being normal. For broadcast purposes, prefer NORMALITY, because it is the more commonly used.

Not Guilty   *See* **Innocent**.

Notorious   *See* **Famous**.   Note spelling—it is not nortorious.

Noxious   *See* **Noisome**.

Nuclear   Pronounce it with three syllables: NOO-klee-uhr.

Nutritional/Nutritious   Related but not synonymous. *NUTRITIONAL* has to do with the mechanism by which living things take in nourishment—it refers to the process. *NUTRITIOUS* refers to the nourishment value of that which is taken in.

Observance/Observation   An *OBSERVANCE* usually has to do with a ceremony, the carrying out of a ritual. An *OBSERVATION* is the act of taking notice. However, in certain contexts, observation can be used as a synonym for observance.

Occupation/Vocation   Not every OCCUPATION is a VOCATION, although, as in so many other cases, the words are frequently treated as synonyms. An *occupation* is generally seen as the principal work of one's life, so studying can be the occupation of a student. A *vocation* is, as the word implies, a calling—a strong summons to do certain work. Members of the clergy are often said to follow a calling, a vocation. Journalists, too, very often see themselves as "called" to do what they do. Heaven knows, very few of them are in it for the money!

Occur   See **Happen**.

Oculist/Ophthalmologist/Optician/Optometrist   All these folks work with the eyes or eye glasses. An *OCULIST, OPTICIAN*, and *OPTOMETRIST* have varying levels of training and specialize in examination of the eyes and the fitting of eyeglasses. An *OPHTHALMOLOGIST* is a medical doctor who specializes in diseases of the eye, but may also fit eyeglasses.

Official   Not everyone who talks to the media is an OFFICIAL. Policemen, although properly called officers, are not all police officials. An *official* is one who holds an office, especially a public office. Please don't refer to rescue squadsmen or all hospital spokespersons as officials unless they really are.

Off Of/On To   Most often "of" and "to" are unnecessary baggage.

Often   The "T" is silent. Pronounce it OFF-un.

Older   *See* **Elder**.

On/Onto   Test the usage. "The band marched ON the field," and "the band marched ONTO the field," tell entirely different stories.

Only Time Will Tell...   A waffle phrase. So is "We'll just have to wait and see." Avoid them. They have no place in straight news, anyway. "Remains to be seen," it has been pointed out, can be found at a funeral home.

On The Day/Season   Sports people, tell me what this means? It is a vogue phrase and should be avoided by serious writers.

Opossum   Pronounced, y'all, POSS-um. Nawthuners often pronounce the "O". It's silent or nearly so. Whatever sound there is comes closer to "uh" than "oh."

Oral/Verbal   *ORAL* has to do with the mouth, so something spoken can be said to be oral. *VERBAL* has to do with words, written or spoken, but most often written. Just to add to the confusion, we can toss in *AURAL*, which sounds almost like oral but has to do with hearing, of all things. A frequent misuse is in the description of an agreement as a "...verbal contract" when there is no written document. What is meant is "...oral contract."

Ordinance/Ordnance   Watch the spelling closely. *ORDNANCE* is military hardware. An *ORDINANCE* is a law governing a city. Only cities, towns, and counties enact "*ORDINANCES*."

Oregon Favor OAR-eh-gun as the pronunciation.

Oscillate *See* **Alternate.**

Ought *See* **Aught.**

Outside *See* **Inside.**

Over *See* **More Than.**

Pago Pago The capital city of American Samoa is pronounced "PAHNG-o PAHNG-o" no matter how it's spelled.

Paid/Payed/Played A loan is PAID out, a rope is PAYED out, and a drama is PLAYED out. The common error here is to say a rope is played out. If, however, you have run out of rope, it is common to say "the rope has played out."

Palate/Palette/Pallet The *PALATE* is the roof of the mouth, an artist keeps paints on a *PALETTE*, and heavy materials are stacked on a *PALLET* so a forklift can get under them.

Parity/Parody *PARITY* has to do with equality. Broadcasters worry about having First Amendment parity with the print media. A *PARODY* is writing, music or drama in an imitative manner for humorous effect.

Palpate/Palpitate When the doctor thumps on your back, that's *PALPATING*. When your heart goes "pitty-pat" it's *PALPITATING*. To *palpate* is to touch, to feel. To *palpitate* is to quake, tremble, beat faster than normal or irregularly. It usually refers to the heartbeat.

Passed/Past The problem here is in the spelling. *PAST* has numerous meanings and uses, including to go by. *PASSED* is a verb and means only to go by. "The car passed the truck." "The truck roared past."

Pathologist *See* **Coroner.**

Partially/Partly Both have the meaning of not entirely. Prefer PARTLY.

Past Experience A redundancy. All EXPERIENCE is PAST.

Patient Conditions This is a personal bug-a-boo. There are only four patient conditions in a hospital environment. They are "Good," "Fair," "Serious" (or "Poor") and "Critical." There are no such conditions as "Satisfactory" or

"Stable." Stable has come into use only in the past few years and means nothing. The only possible meaning could be that the patient is not getting any worse. To say a patient is in "critical but stable condition" is a contradiction in terms. "Critical condition" means the vital signs are unstable. See Appendix II.

Patron   *See* **Client.**

Peculiar   *See* **Funny.**

Pedal/Peddle/Petal   You *PEDAL* a bicycle, you might *PEDDLE* vegetables on the street—it means to sell informally— and, of course, flowers are made up of PETALS.

Pendulum   Pronounced as if spelled with a "J"—PEN-juh-lum.

Peninsula   Don't say "surrounded on three sides..." *Surround* means completely around. A *PENINSULA* is bounded on three sides, usually by water. It is pronounced pe-NIN-sulah—not pen-INCH-ulah.

Penitentiary   *See* **Jail.**

People/Persons   *PEOPLE* is not always the plural of *person* and neither is *PERSONS*. Use *persons* as the plural when you are speaking a specific number of individuals—no matter how large a number, but use *PEOPLE* when the number is indefinite. "Three persons were injured in the crash." "The people of New York continue to flock to Yankees games."

Per/Via   Avoid the Latinates. Miles an hour, came by truck are just fine.

Percent   Write it as one word.

Perfect   In its most common use, *PERFECT* means flawless. If so, can it be qualified? One of our national treasures speaks of forming "a more perfect union." In most uses, however, keep it unqualifiable.

Perfunctory   Note the spelling, it is not "PRE," it is "PER." It means something done only as a duty or superficially. It's a terrible word for broadcast.

Perish   *See* **Die.**

Perquisite/Prerequisite   Don't get confused. A *PERQUISITE*— the beloved "perks" of certain occupations—is a privilege, such as a company car or extra fees. A *PREREQUISITE* is a requirement in advance. You must have Introduction to Reporting as a prerequisite to Advanced Reporting.

Persecute/Prosecute *PERSECUTE* means to follow or hunt down, to harass. *PROSECUTE* means to bring to trial, in modern usage. Another use is in the sense of to follow to completion.

Perspiration Note that it is not PRESS-pur-ay-shun. It is PUR-spu-ray-shun. It is a euphemism. Use "sweat."

Phase *See* **Faze**.

Philippines *See* **Filipino**.

Pidgin English "PIDGIN" is an artifical language mostly found in the South Pacific. It has nothing to do with the bird—it's not even spelled like "pigeon." It's thought *pidgin* is a pidgin word for *business*, because that's why the language was developed—so people could deal with each other even though they didn't speak the same language. It is not always associated with English, although it borrows heavily from it. Pidgin (or in pidgin, tok-pisin) is the official government and business language of Papua New Guinea and there is a major government effort to get all citizens to use it.

Pimiento The red stuff in green olives. Regardless of how it's spelled, it's pronounced puh-MENT-oe.

Pincers A military maneuver in which one army is surrounded by another. It is always expressed as a plural. It is pronounced PIN-serz, not PINCH-erz.

Pistol *See* **Automatic**.

Pizza Pie A redundancy, PIZZA is a pie.

Plaintiff/Plaintive You need to be careful with the pronunciation here. A *PLAINTIFF* is one who has a complaint against someone else—it is usually associated with civil court cases. *PLAINTIVE* is an adjective expressing sadness, melancholy. The two words are related through "plaint" which has a use in law as well as meaning an utterance of lamentation.

Pleaded/Pled *PLED* until recently was considered nonstandard English. For broadcast use PLEADED.

Plurality *See* **Majority**.

Plus Avoid using *PLUS* as a conjuction, as in "He is a careful driver plus a good mechanic."

Podium *See* **Dais**.

Poinsettia The latest dictionaries (at least some of them) now say the preferred pronunciation of this showy Christmastime plant is poyn-SET-uh. That pleases me, because that's the way I've always said it. Other dictionaries, however, insist that not only is poyn-SET-ee-uh preferred, it is the only pronunciation. It certainly is spelled for the four-syllable treatment.

Police Among other things, be careful with the pronunication. It is puh-LEES, not PLEES or POH-lees.

Pore/Pour You PORE over a book, but POUR a cup of coffee.

Port *See* **Harbor**.

Posthumous It means after life ends and is pronounced PAHS-choo-muhs.

Post Mortem *See* **Autopsy**.

Potpourri A mixture, specifically of herbs and flowers, but used to describe any conglomeration of dissimilar things. It comes from the French and is pronounced poh-puh-REE, in English.

Practically/Almost *PRACTICALLY* means for all practical purposes—as in the bucket is practically empty. It also has the sense of ALMOST. For broadcast, use almost.

Practice *See* **Habit**.

Pray/Prey Today, *PRAY* almost always has the sense of imploring a diety. *PREY* is something that is hunted. The insect is a "praying mantis" because of the attitude of its forelegs, even though it is a voracious predator.

Precipitate/Precipitous *PRECIPTATE* means to fall out of or to cause. *PRECIPITOUS* means with a lack of caution, to act in haste.

Preferable Pronounced PREF-eh-ruh-buhl.

Prefixes Hyphenate freely, especially to breakup vowel strings as in co-operate, anti-aircraft, re-election and co-education.

Prelude How do we pronounce this familiar word? Well, it seems there are several ways, Dictionaries give at least five versions: PRELL-ood, PRELL-yood, PRAY-lood, PRAY-lyood, PRE-lood and so on, depending on the sense in which it is used. Primarily, *PRELUDE* means something that comes before the main action, preparing for what is to come, usually in music. The use has become extended to include nearly anything that precedes something else.

Premature   See **Immature**.

Prerecorded   A seeming nonsense word; after all, something cannot be post-recorded. But it is a useful word in the phrase "Parts of the preceding were prerecorded." To say "Parts of the preceding were recorded" could have an entirely different meaning. However, for the sake of precision, I still prefer the latter.

Prescribe/Proscribe   Look-alikes that have entirely different meanings. To *PRESCRIBE* is to direct that something be done. To *PROSCRIBE* is to forbid the doing of something.

Present   Be careful of creating redundancies such as "the present incumbent."

Presently   *See* **Currently**.

Presume   *See* **Assume**.

Pretense/Pretext   A *PRETENSE* is, as the word implies, the act of pretending—an action intended to deceive. A *PRETEXT* is an excuse. The words are closely similar; some dictionaries say they are synonymous.

Price Hike   Please avoid using HIKE or similar words when you mean "increase." It's a headline word that has no place in working English in that sense.

Principal/Principle   These are distantly related words that are often confused. *PRINCIPAL* means foremost, the chief, the one who holds a leading position—the high school principal. *PRINCIPLE* refers to a basic law or truth, a rule. Both words have other more narrow meanings. It's best to consult a dictionary when it doubt.

Prison   *See* **Jail**.

Prisoner   *See* **Convict**.

Problematic   If a thing is said to be *PROBLEMATIC* it means it is in doubt—not necessarily that there is a problem with it.

Produce *PRODUCE* has two distinctly different meanings and three different pronunciations. *Produce* (pronounced PRAWD-oos or PROHD-oos) refers to a product, usually a farm product, most often fruit and vegetables. *Produce* (pronounced pruh-DOOS) means to manufacture, to create, or bring to light.

Prognosis *See* **Diagnosis**.

Prostate/Prostrate *PROSTATE* is the very useful, but often troublesome gland in males. To be *PROSTRATE* is to be lying horizontally in submission or, metaphorically, to be helpless or in a humble position.

Protein Note spelling; it is pronounced PROH-teen.

Prototype Model A redundancy; a *PROTOTYPE* is a *MODEL*. It is, in fact, a first model.

Proved/Proven Both are acceptable as past tenses of "prove." For broadcast, *PROVEN* is to be preferred in most instances.

Psychiatrist/Psychologist A *PSYCHIATRIST* is a medical doctor who practices psychiatry. A *PSYCHOLOGIST* is a student of the mind, one who practices counselling or clinical psychology. A psychologist may be a medical doctor but most often is not.

Pupil/Student Although dictionaries say PUPIL and STUDENT are synonyms, usage dictates a distinction. Use *pupil* when referring to a young student—usually in elementary school. High school and college inmates are called *students*.

Puzzle *See* **Enigma**.

Quantum It has become fashionable to characterize anything that increases or moves forward as having taken a QUANTUM leap or some other such verb. *Quantum* has distinct meanings in physics, but in the language of the rest of us it refers to bulk or gross quantity. It is possible to have a tiny quantum of something. Avoid the word.

Quart/Quarter   Watch your pronunciation of these. Why is it people who can pronounce "quartz" just fine, will pronunce QUART as KORT every time? It's KWORT and KWORT-ur.

Quebec   The province in eastern Canada is pronounced kweh-BEK.

Question   *See* **Inquiry**.

Rabid   The state of having rabies. Do not speak of a RABID sports fan. What you mean is avid.

Raffle Off   The OFF is unnecessary.

Rainfall   *See* **Weather Words**.

Raise/Rear   Some authorities are surrendering on this one, but the purists hang on. You *REAR* children, but *RAISE* other things.

Ration   The preferred pronunciation is RASH-uhn. RAY-shun is acceptable.

Ravage/Ravish   *RAVAGE* means to ruin, destroy; violent devastation. *RAVISH* means to carry away or kidnap, usually a woman, with rape in mind; but, oddly, *ravishing* means having great beauty or attractiveness when used as an adjective.

Reaction/Response   A *REACTION* is an unthinking, spontaneous response to a stimulus. A *RESPONSE* is any action brought on by a stimulus, but for our purposes, limit it to a thought-out answer, or other action. Therefore, an answer to criticism by a politician is not a reaction, but rather, a response.

Readable   *See* **Legible**.

Realtor   A member of the National Association of Realtors—not just someone who happens to sell real estate.

Rebellion/Revolution/Revolt   There's a difference. Why do we call it the American (or French) REVOLUTION, but the Boxer REBELLION? Because a *revolution* (a turning around) is a rebellion that was successful. A rebellion usually does not succeed. A *rebellion* is open defiance of authority, but not necessarily wih the intent of overthrowing that authority. *REVOLT* also comes from the idea of turning over and means a turning away from established authority or rule.

Rebut/Refute   *REBUT* in common use means to oppose by legal argument, to counter another's claim. *REFUTE* means to bring forth evidence or logic to overthrow another's claim and prove it wrong. A rebuttal may not be convincing and successful; a refutation is.

Record   When one sets a RECORD that's it, it is not a new record.

Red-Haired/Red-Headed   Prefer RED-HAIRED when referring to people. It is a RED-HEADED woodpecker, however.

Referee/Umpire   Generally used synonymously with the sense of judging. Commonly, usage depends on the sport involved. Baseball has UMPIRES, football and boxing have REFEREES, for example. Both terms are used outside sports, as well. There are, for example, referees in bankruptcy and umpired art shows.

Regina   The capital city of Saskatchewan is pronounced ruh-JY-nuh.

Reign/Rein   A monarch has a *REIGN*, a horse is controlled by a *REIN*. To give one "free rein" is to set him or her free to do as he or she will. It is not "free reign," although that would seem to carry the same idea.

Relic   A *RELIC* is, by definition, old. "Old relic" is a redundancy. So is "old tradition" or "long-standing tradition."

Reluctant/Reticent   *RELUCTANT* means unwilling or hesitant to act. *RETICENT* means unwilling or hesitant to speak. *Reticence* has to do only with restraint in expression or communication.

Rend/Render   To *REND* is to tear or split violently. To *RENDER* is to reduce, melt down, such as animal fat is rendered into lard. *Render* also has many other meanings, the most common being to reduce to helplessness, to render unconscious. A touching scene is heartrending not heartrendering.

Rent   *See* **Lease**.

Reparable   Capable of being fixed. It is pronounced REP-ur-uhbl.

Repeat Again A redundancy, *REPEAT* means to do it *AGAIN*.

Replenish Yes, the word meaning to resupply or to fill is related through its Latin root to "plenty," but there's no "t" in it. Pronounce it ree-PLEHN-ish.

Replete This is a word more often misused than not. *REPLETE* means to have something in great abundance—it does not have the sense of being complete, even though it sounds as though it does. A recent advertisement informed us that an apartment was "replete with a microwave oven and stove." A correct usage would be "Iowa farms are replete with corn." With always accompanies replete.

Replica *See* **Copy**.

Reported/Reputed Take away the "ED" endings and you will readily see the difference. *REPORTED* means the transmission of information, the telling of the story. Reportedly has come into use as a substitute for REPUTED. *Repute* has to do with reputation or esteem, which can be either high or low. The use of reputed for reported may result from a confusion with putative, which is a related word and means assumed to be true or accepted as fact.

Reprise Pronounced ruh-PREEZ.

Repugnant/Repulsive *REPUGNANT* means to be opposed to, incompatible. *REPULSIVE* means disgusting, repelling.

Reputable Pronounced REP-yuht-uh-buhl.

Reside *See* **Dwell**.

Restaurateur One who owns or operates a restaurant. Note the spelling and the pronunciation. There is no "n" as there is in restaurant. It is Rehs-tuh-ruh-TOOR.

Restive/Restless *RESTIVE* means stubborn, unwilling to submit to authority, inflexible. *RESTLESS* has to do with discontent, or constant motion, nervousness.

Retch/Wretch To *RETCH* is to gag or throw up, to vomit, actually the heaving action just before vomiting. A *WRETCH* is a pitiable person, one who lives in degradation.

Revolve *See* **Center On**.

Revolver   *See* **Automatic.**

Richter Scale   *See* **Earthquake.**

Riddle   *See* **Enigma.**

Rile/Roil   There is a close relationship between RILE and ROIL. Some authorities consider them synonymous. For precision, however, there is a distinction to be drawn. *Rile* means to stir up emotionally, to make angry. *Roil* means to stir up physically, to turn a liquid cloudy; by roiling the muddy bottom of a pond, for example.

Rio   "RIO" means river. Don't write "the Rio Grande River." "Rio Grande" means big river.

Risk   *See* **Weather Words.**

Robbery   *See* **Burglary.**

Route   Pronounce it ROOT.

Ruffed Grouse   The game bird is a RUFFED grouse—not ruffled.

Rug   *See* **Carpet.**

Sahara   *SAHARA* means desert. Refer to "The Sahara" not "the Sahara Desert."

SALT Treaty   A redundancy. *SALT* is the acronym for Strategic Arms Limitation Treaty. To say SALT Treaty you are saying Treaty twice. You need to watch acronyms closely for this trap.

Sanatarium/Sanatorium   Note spellings —it is SANA, not SANI. These are probably the same thing, but usage has brought a distinction. A *SANATARIUM* is a facility for housing the mentally ill. A *SANATORIUM* is a facility for housing those with other chronic illnesses, such as tuberculosis. It is a fine distinction and probably not important. What is important is knowing how the institution in your story refers to itself.

Saving/Savings   You put your money in a SAVINGS account, but it is Daylight SAVING Time. No final "S."

Scared/Scarred   A frequent spelling error that can really foul a news program. Be careful.

Scare Words Its difficult in this day and time to think of SCARE WORDS—words that in themselves can cause panic. There are a few, however. Be very careful with epidemic, tornado, riot, things to do with escaped dangerous criminals, lunatics and so on. Report the events, of course, but do not unnecessarily stir up the populace— unless, of course, there is imminent danger—such as the local dam about to burst. In that case, panic is the order of the day.

Scholar Today, a *SCHOLAR* is usually found at a university and is someone who has obtained a great depth of knowledge in a particular field.

Score *See* **Margin**.

Scotch/Scots/Scottish Anyone with a name such as mine gets sensitive about the misuse of these words. First, please don't use SCOTCH to mean cheap. That's plain offensive. *SCOTCH* refers to the whisky and other products of Scotland. The people, although not objecting to being called *Scotch* are properly referred to as the *SCOTS* or *SCOTTISH*. *Scottish* also refers to all things having to do with Scotland. *Scotch* also has the informal meaning of to quell, such as a rumor.

Scrip/Script *Scrip* is the paper currency issued following an emergency when the basic economy has been wrecked; a war is a good example of such an emergency. A *SCRIPT* is, among other things, what broadcast newswriters create several times a day.

Sculpt/Sculptor/Sculpture To *SCULPT* is to create a *SCULP-TURE*. The one who does it is a *SCULPTOR*.

Seasonable/Seasonal Something that is *SEASONABLE* is typical of the season. Temperatures are said to be seasonable. Something that is *SEASONAL* varies with the season. Skiing is a seasonal sport.

Secondly *See* **Firstly**.

Sensual/Sensuous *SENSUAL* carries a sense of gratification of the senses and usually is used to relate to sexual attractiveness. *SENSUOUS* has a more aesthetic sense, to be inwardly appreciative of such things as art and music.

Septic *See* **Antiseptic**.

Service *See* **Mass**.

Sewage/Sewerage The network of pipes and pumps that takes care of a city's waste is called a *SEWERAGE* system. The stuff that flows through the system is called *SEWAGE*. Thus the sewage treatment plant is the last stop in the sewerage system.

Sex *See* **Gender**.

Ship *See* **Boat**.

Sick *See* **Ill**.

Sierra *SIERRA* means a type of mountains and it is plural. It is the Sierra Nevada not the Sierra Nevadas or Sierra Nevada Mountains. On second reference, however, The Sierras is considered proper.

Sight *See* **Cite**.

Simultaneous *See* **Coincident**.

Since *See* **Because**.

Site *See* **Cite**.

Skeptic *See* **Cynic**.

Slew/Slough In most senses, these are pronounced SLOO. SLEW always is. It means to swerve or skid around—as an automobile does on ice. *SLOUGH* is pronounced SLOO when it refers to a swamp or mire, which is the usual meaning. However, peeling skin—such as following a bad sunburn—is said to slough off, and in that case, it is pronounced SLUFF.

Small-Businessman Always hyphenate so as to make clear that SMALL refers to the size of the business and not the size of the man.

Sniper A *SNIPER* is a gunman who shoots from concealment at an exposed enemy. I do not think it is correct to refer to a police sniper in a hostage situation where an officer shoots the hostage taker. Call the officer a police sharp-shooter. *Sniper* has a negative connotation.

Socks/Stockings *SOCKS* are generally considered to be short foot coverings, reaching mid-calf. *STOCKINGS* in common use refer to long foot and leg coverings worn primarily by women. However, anyone—man or woman—who is without shoes is said to be in stocking feet.

Sordid   *See* **Morbid.**

Specie/Species   *SPECIE* usually pronounced SPEE-she, refers to coins—money. *SPECIES* pronounced either SPEE-sheez or SPEE-seez, refers to a biological type, a variety of life.

Spectators   *See* **Audience.**

Spitting Image   This somewhat vulgar, but colorful phrase is also seen as "The spit and image." It means an exact likeness and is often used to compare a child to a parent.

Spree   Usually avoid *SPREE* in reference to a series of crimes. The word means overindulgence or an outburst of any activity, but usually it carries the idea of having fun. I don't think a person engaged in several killings is having much fun.

Stanch/Staunch   *STANCH* means to stop the flow. We speak of "stanching" blood. Note that the idea of stopping a flow is built into the word, so to say "stanching the flow of blood" is redundant, although commonly heard. To be *STAUNCH* is to be steadfast, loyal, strongly supportive.

State Of. . .   Needed only when referring to Washington or New York to differentiate from the cities of the same name. In other cases, just name the state.

Stationary/Stationery   There is a slight variation in pronunciation between *STATIONARY*—at a standstill, unmoving —and *STATIONERY*—writing materials and office supplies. The final vowel sound in stationary is -airy, while in stationery it is -erry. The difference is slight.

Straight/Strait   We all know the many meanings of STRAIGHT. Note the different spelling of *STRAIT*—a narrow body of water between two land masses—the Strait of Gibraltar, Torres Strait.

Straitjacket   The word *STRAITJACKET* refers to a restraining device. Note the spelling of trait.

Strangle/Strangulate   These both have the same basic meaning —to cut off the air supply until death results. *STRAN-*

GULATE has a broader meaning in medical circles, where a strangulated hernia is so swollen that the blood supply to the tissue is cut off and the tissue dies.

Strangled To Death   A redundancy. *See* **Strangle**.

Strategy/Tactics   A *STRATEGY* is a master plan either military or not. *TACTICS* are part of that plan—how one goes about achieving the goals of the plan.

Student   *See* **Pupil**.

Subsequent   *See* **Consequent**.

Successive   *See* **Consecutive**.

Such As   *See* **Like**.

Suicide   Be careful in SUICIDE stories not to write what is probably a non sequitur—"He died of self-inflicted wounds." It's very unlikely there would be more than one wound.

Suit/Suite   Both mean set or group. *SUIT* usually refers to clothing, except in court or on a card table, and is pronounced SOOT. *SUITE* is often used to refer to a set of musical compositions or groups of rooms or furniture and is pronounced SWEET. *Suit* has numerous additional uses. See your dictionary.

Suppress/Surpress   *SUPPRESS* means to conceal or hold back. There is no such word as *SURPRESS*, which we often hear when the speaker wants *suppress*. It probably derives from the word being so similar to *surprise*.

Surprise   *See* **Astonish**.

Suspected   *See* **Accused**.

Sustain   A favorite word of the writers of accident stories. *SUSTAIN* means to survive, to withstand. Therefore, "He died of injuries sustained in the crash" is nonsense. If he sustained the injuries, he survived. Sustain does not have the same meaning as suffered or received.

Swimsuit   *See* **Bathing Suit**.

Take   *See* **Bring**.

Tarmac   The paved area in front of an airport terminal or hangar is called the *TARMAC*. It's really short for tarmacadam, a trade name for a certain kind of paving developed by Scottish engineer John MacAdam early in the 19th century. The term does not apply generally to airport pavement—only the apron near the terminal or hangar, taxi-ways and perhaps runways.

Teen-Age Dictionaries recognize *TEENAGED* as a secondary spelling, but please don't use it. The term is always hyphenated in broadcast copy. See the discussion under *BOY/MAN*.

Telephone Poll A poll taken by telephone is probably properly called a *TELEPHONE POLL*, but that's really confusing. Try to find a better way to describe it. Call it a "survey."

Temblor *See* **Earthquake**.

Temperature *See* **Fever**.

Tennessee *See* **Detroit**.

Tenterhooks When one is anxiously awaiting something, or is uneasy, one is said to be on TENTERHOOKS. The word is often jocularly pronounced *tenderhooks*. A tenter is a wooden frame on which fabric is stretched. It has many small sharp nails around the perimeter to hold the fabric. They are called tenterhooks. So the image is of one so strained that he or she is stretched on a frame.

Test out The "OUT" is unnecessary.

That THAT causes problems. Broadcasters should avoid the excessive use of *that*. Too many *thats* create a "machine-gun" effect: That-a-that-that. Test each sentence in which that appears to see whether it might read just as well and mean the same thing without the *that*. Most of the time *that* can be left out without damaging the sense of what you are trying to say. "The Prime Minister said that the Navy is in full alert." "The Prime Minister said the Navy is in full alert." There are times, however, when *that* is needed for clarity, in which cases, of course, leave it in.

That/Which/Who This one puzzles even the best of writers. My way of handling which word to use is to decide whether the phrase being introduced is to be set off by commas or parentheses. If the setting off is needed, then use *WHICH*. If it will not be set off (that is, the phrase is necessary for the understanding of the sentence) then use *THAT*. There are formal rules of grammar that give you the technicalities, but I think my way works fine. By the way, *which* normally refers to things, while *that* refers to people or things, and *who* only to people. I find referring to a person as *that* to be grating.

Think   *See* **Feel**.

Thoroughbred   Only horses are *THOROUGHBREDS*. It is a specific breed of race and show horse. The word is used informally to describe other domestic animals and sometimes people.

Threat   *See* **Weather Words**.

To All Intensive Purposes   One of many gaffes to show up on student term papers and quizzes. Another of my favorites is "It's a doggy dog world." Ranking close behind is "Fair to midland." What the writers were after, respectively, was "To all intents and purposes," "it's a dog-eat-dog world" and "fair to middling."

Toddler   *See* **Baby**.

Tomato   Where you come from plays a large part in what you call this fruit (it is a fruit, by the way, not a vegetable). I believe the only correct pronunciation is tuh-MAYT-oh, because that's the way I say it. A close associate of mine calls it a tuh-MAWT-oh. Some people would say that's affected. My mother persisted in calling it a tuh-MAT-oh, which may be limited to a now-abandoned lumbering town at Lincoln Gap, Vermont, where she spent a number of her formative years.

Tornado   *See* **Cyclone**.

Tortuous/Torturous   A *TORTUOUS* road is one that has many twists and bends. The word also refers to anything that is devious. There is usually a connotation of danger inherent in the word. *TORTUROUS* has to do with torture—physical abuse.

Totalled The Car   This is an informal phrase at best. It means damage was so great the cost of repair would be more than the value of the vehicle, so damage was declared total.

Toward   *See* **Afterward**.

Tract   *See* **Acre**.

Trademarks and Names   We frequently find the need to refer to things in the news that are familiarly called by their trade names. We must keep in mind that these names are valuable property and should not be used as generic names for those sorts of things. I refer to calling all photocopiers "Xerox" machines, all plastic tape "Scotch" tape, all tissues "Kleenex," and so on. If these trade names become generic, they are lost to the owner. There are many cases in which that has happened. The media play a large role in either retaining the owner's interest or helping him or her lose it. Other examples that come immediately to mind are: TV Guide, Coke and Coca Cola, Popsicle, Tabasco, Day-Glo, Caterpillar, Cook's Tour, Rolodex, Weight Watchers, Velcro, Vise-Grip, Frigidaire, Breathalizer, TelePromTer and Heatilator. There are many others.

Transpire   *See* **Happen**.

Treachery/Treason   *TREACHERY* is a violation of trust or confidence; to cheat. We usually think of treachery as being serious business. *TREASON* is usually used to indicate treachery against one's country. It is, under certain circumstances, punishable by death.

Triumphal/Triumphant   A celebration following a victory of some sort can be referred to as TRIUMPHAL. The person basking in the glow of victory is said to be TRIUMPHANT.

Troop/Troops/Troupe   When referring to military men, the reference is always to *TROOPS*, it is not used as a singular. *TROOP* used to refer to a unit of mounted cavalry equivalent to a company of foot soldiers. *Troop* has a number of other meanings as well. Actors come in TROUPES.

Trustee/Trusty   Take care with this, trusty reader. They are frequently confused and therefore misused. A *TRUSTEE* (pronounced truss-TEE) is a person who has been given a great deal of responsibility over the funds or affairs of others. A trustee of a bank, for example, or a member of a university's board of trustees. A *TRUSTY* is a prisoner who, because of good behavior, is given a certain degree of freedom in exchange for peforming some jail house tasks. It is pronounced TRUSS-tee. *Trusty* also means faithful, trustworthy, as in "my trusty rifle."

Try And/Try To   TRY AND implies two actions. I will try and I will do. Most of the time you will want TRY TO. But, if you indeed do have two things in mind, then of course use *try and.*

Turbid/Turgid   *TURBID* means cloudy, impure, polluted. Water than has been roiled (see **Rile**) is turbid and so is air filled with smoke. *TURGID* (pronounced TER-jid) means swollen or distended or when referring to writing style, overly embellished, pompous.

Two in a Row   This can't be. It takes three, at least, to make a row. To say "Temperatures will top 90 degrees for the second day in a row" makes no sense.

Typhoon   *See* **Cyclone.**

Umpire   *See* **Referee.**

Underweigh/-Way   The term is nautical in origin—it means to have weighed (hoisted) the anchor and to be moving. Today's usage, however, has it spelled *UNDERWAY*, which makes more sense when speaking of anything but boats.

Uninterested   *See* **Disinterested**.

Unique   *UNIQUE* is one of those words, such as "pregnant," that cannot be qualified. Something is one of a kind or it's not. Very unique or nearly unique are just plain wrong.

University   *See* **College**.

Unloosen/Unravel   These look wrong, but they are correct. For some reason we often seem to need two words that mean the same thing. *UNLOOSEN* means to loosen. *UNRAVEL* means to ravel. *Unloosen* and *unravel* seem to carry the sense of deliberate acts, while *loosen* and *ravel* are accidental or occur spontaneously—I think.

-up   Almost never needed, as in "fix-up," "warmed up," "catch up," and so on. Test each *"-UP"* to see if you can live without it.

Up-Coming A redundancy to be avoided.

Uppermost/Upmost/Utmost Although *UPMOST* is a perfectly good word, meaning of the highest rank or order, use *UPPERMOST*, which means the same thing and avoids confusing the sense with that of UTMOST, which means most extreme, at the farthest point, of the highest degree of intensity: "Of the utmost importance."

Urgent *See* **Wire Services**.

Use/Utilize Generally, *UTILIZE* is to be considered pretentious and avoided in broadcast copy. There are times, though, when USE just doesn't make the grade. In such cases, use utilize.

Utility Pole Instead of guessing what it was the car ran into—use "UTILITY POLE" rather than power pole or telephone pole. Actually, it's a rare pole these days that does not carry several different kinds of cable and wires.

Uttering *See* **Forging**.

Vacant *See* **Empty**.

Vacuum Note the spelling—one C, two Us. It is pronounced with three syllables—VAK-yoo-um.

Vascillate *See* **Alternate**.

VDT Terminal The same sort of redundancy we encountered with SALT Treaty. The acronym VDT means Video Display Terminal. You don't want to say terminal twice, do you?

Vehicle The "H" is silent. Pronounce it VEE-ik-uhl.

Verbal *See* **Oral**.

Veritable/Virtual *VERITABLE* has to do with verity, truth. It means actual, not false, the thing actually named. It is often confused with *VIRTUAL*, which means to be functionally or effectively something—"virtually the same as sugar."

Vermont *See* **Detroit**.

Via *See* **Per**.

Vis-A-Vis Literally, face-to-face. A useful French phrase for comparing opposites or likenesses. Pronounced VEEZ-ah-VEE.

Vocation *See* **Occupation**.

Wackey Related to whacky but not spelled or pronounced that way. It means pretty much the same thing—erratic, silly. Whacky comes from "whack-head, someone who's been stupified by a blow to the head or punch-drunk.

Wait For/Wait On If your sense is to be awaiting something or someone, use *WAIT FOR*. "Wait for me on the corner." If your sense is of service to another, then use *WAIT ON*. "He waits on her hand and foot."

Wane/Wax These terms are frequently found in referring to the phases of the moon, but are figuratively used to express the idea of gradual coming and going. *WANE* means to slowly fade away, while *WAX* means to gradually increase. Do not confuse wane with wan (pronounced WAWN) which means pale, sallow.

Was a Former... As long as a person is alive, he or she remains a former of whatever he or she was. To say a living person WAS A FORMER Senator, for example, is to imply that he or she is dead.

Washington *See* **State Of**....

Weather Words Some of these terms already have been discussed, but we'll look at them again. The forecast from the Weather Service (whatever it's called now) in Winter will often include the term *bitterly cold*. That's about as subjective as one can get. In fact, the terms *hot* and *cold* mean very different things in different parts of the country and at different times of year. *Bitter* has, as one sense, harsh, causing discomfort or pain. I guess that's what "bitter cold" means. Once again, *currently* and *presently* do not mean the same thing. Do not say "the temperature is presently 60 degrees." *Presently* means soon. *Cyclone, hurricane, tornado* and *typhoon* have already been discussed—look under **Cyclone**. Even though the Weather Service people may refer to forecasting as *progging*, please resist the temptation. It is jargon and should be avoided. *See* Chap 2, The Weather, for a discussion of rainfall. *See* also **Seasonable**. I object to weather people referring to a *threat* or *risk* of some weather feature. It's a natural phenomenon and rarely is there any great danger. If the air is not moving, there is no wind. Avoid saying "the wind is calm." That's a contradiction in terms. If the wind is blowing, there is a chill factor involved. That is the effect of wind on the skin, making the effective temperature lower than that measured by a thermometer. Do not say "the wind-chill factor is minus three degrees." Say "with the wind-chill factor, the temperature is minus three degrees." Do you know what POP is? It is the Probability Of Precipitation. Do you know what that means? Most people don't. It is expressed as a percentage and it means the likelihood of rain or snow. It is derived from computer analysis of weather data over a 100-year period. When this particular set of weather conditions has existed in the past, it has brought on rain this percentage of the time. It does not mean it will rain that percentage of the day, nor over that percentage of the area. Please don't say, as the official forecast will, "a near-zero percent chance of precipitation." That sounds awful. Just leave it out. There are three levels of severe weather notices used by the Weather Service. They are from least to most urgent: *Watch, Warning,* and *Alert.* Watch means that conditions are right for certain kinds of severe weather to develop; Warning means that the severe weather has been sighted nearby; Alert means it is almost certain the severe weather will be upon us soon. You should be very careful to use the proper level in any story related to severe weather, perhaps even explaining what they mean.

To give you an idea of how necessary it is to translate what comes out of the weather bureau, the following is an exact quotation from a severe weather warning as sent from the Weather Service to the Associated Press:

"THE SEVERE THUNDERSTORM WATCH AREA IS ALONG AND 70 STATUTE MILES EITHER SIDE OF A LINE FROM 45 MILES SOUTH OF FLORENCE SOUTH CAROLINA TO 35 MILES EAST OF RICHMOND VIRGINIA."

I defy anyone without a map to refer to, to explain

where the watch area is. The frightening thing about this is the AP sent it exactly as it was received.

Weapon *See* **Automatic**.

Wench/Winch This confusion occurs too often to be mere accident. A *WENCH* is an old word meaning peasant girl or serving girl. It is now used only humorously. A *WINCH* is a device containing a spool of cable or rope used to lift or pull heavy things.

Whereabouts Is treated as a singular. "His WHEREABOUTS is unknown."

Whether *See* **If**.

Which *See* **That/Which**

Whiskey/Whisky If it is Scotch it is WHISKY, if it is any other kind it is WHISKEY. Both are pronounced the same.

Wide *See* **Broad**.

Widow In stories involving the death of a man say "he leaves his wife," not his WIDOW. She's the widow, all right, but when he left, she was his wife.

Wind *See* **Weather Words**.

Wind Chill Factor *See* **Weather Words**.

Windfall A *WINDFALL* is a surprise good fortune. Originally, it referred to (and still does in some places) tree branches blown down by wind which became free firewood for those willing to pick them up. Today, a *windfall* can be any unexpected benefit. Unexpected windfall is a redundancy.

Wire Services Special features of the wire services were discussed in Chapter Three. It is important that a broadcast news writer be familiar with the ins and outs of wire service operations and what comes into the newsroom from them. It is also important to know how to perform routine maintenance on the wire service printers—inserting fresh paper supplies and changing ribbons. That sounds a bit infantile, but if you're all by yourself at 5 a.m. and find the machine jammed up, you'll understand what I'm talking about.

Woman *See* **Lady**.

Wounded *See* **Damaged**.

Wrack/Wreak/Wreck Although colorful, the phrase "WRACK and ruin" is a redundancy. *Wrack* means ruin, destruction, violent damage. *WREAK* (pronounced REEK) means to bring down punishment, to indulge in a violent manner, to bring about harm. We all know what a WRECK is.

Xerox *See* **Trademarks**. You know its pronounced ZEER-ocks, don't you?

X-Ray It is pronounced as written—not EX-UH-RAY. Always hyphenate.

Yankee There is some confusion over just what constitutes a YANKEE. Being one from the Deep North, I have more than a passing interest. Somewhere years ago, I read a definition that I believe to be accurate: "Elsewhere in the world, a Yankee is someone from the United States; in the United States, a Yankee is someone from north of the Mason-Dixon Line. North of the line, it is someone from New England. In New England, a Yankee is someone from Vermont and in Vermont a Yankee is a person who has pie for breakfast." A Vermonter would find that amusing. No one else, however.

Yoke/Yolk A *YOKE* is part of a harness used with oxen that functions much the same as a horse collar does. It is usually wooden. There are also *yokes* designed to make it easier for humans to carry heavy loads, although I haven't seen one in years outside museums. *YOLK* is the yellow part of a chicken egg. The color varies with other kinds of fowl.

Youth *See* **Boy**.

Zoom *ZOOM* implies an upward motion—a jet plane zooms to its cruising altitude. It is technically incorrect, although frequently heard, to say the eagle zoomed down on its prey. In broadcasting, *zoom* has its own meaning: to re-

focus a camera lens either "in" or "out," changing the
size of the image.

Zucchini   The ubiquitous dark green summer squash, as everyone probably knows. The word, pronounced zoo-KEE-nee
does provide some important insights into the pronunciation of vowels and consonants in Italian. Most Italian
(and many other) words that end with a vowel receive
stress on the next-to-last syllable. Vowels normally
receive their "natural" sound: U = OO, I = EE, E = EH,
A = AW, O = OH. There is no K in the Italian alphabet.
The sound is achieved by the spelling CCH or CH. The
CH sound is spelled simply C followed by a vowel. The
family name Cecchini is pronounced cheh-KEEN-ee.
Ciao, baby!

APPENDIXES

Police "10-Code"

Law enforcement agencies at all levels across the nation make use of this "10-Code." The 100 entries encompass most of the things police get involved in as well as routine messages. The 10-Code is used to speed communications and to standardize messages.

10-0	Caution	10-19	Return to...
10-1	Unable to copy—move	10-20	Location
10-2	Signal good	10-21	Call...by telephone
10-3	Stop transmitting	10-22	Disregard
10-4	OK (acknowledgement)	10-23	Arrived at scene
10-5	Relay	10-24	Assignment completed
10-6	Busy—stand by	10-25	Report in person (meet)
10-7	Out of service	10-26	Detaining subject
10-8	In service	10-27	License information
10-9	Repeat	10-28	Vehicle registration
10-10	Fight in progress	10-29	Check record for wanted
10-11	Dog case		
10-12	Stand by (stop)	10-30	Illegal use of radio
10-13	Weather/road report	10-31	Crime in progress
10-14	Prowler report	10-32	Man with gun
10-15	Civil disturbance	10-33	EMERGENCY
10-16	Domestic problem	10-34	Riot
10-17	Meet complainant	10-35	Major crime alert
10-18	Complete assignment	10-36	Correct time

10-37	Suspicious vehicle	10-62	Reply to message
10-38	Stopping suspicious vehicle	10-63	Make written copy
10-39	Urgent, use light, siren	10-64	Message for local delivery
10-40	Silent run, no light, siren	10-65	Net message assignment
10-41	Beginning duty tour	10-66	Message cancellation
10-42	Ending duty tour	10-67	Clear for net message
10-43	Information	10-68	Dispatch information
10-44	Request permission to leave patrol for. . .	10-69	Message received
10-45	Animal carcass at. . .	10-70	Fire alarm
		10-71	Advise nature of fire
10-46	Assist motorist	10-72	Report progress of fire
10-47	Need emergency road repair	10-73	Smoke report
		10-74	Negative
10-48	Traffic standard needs repair	10-75	In contact with . . .
		10-76	En route
10-49	Traffic light out at. . .	10-77	ETA (Estimated Time of Arrival)
10-50	Accident (F, PI, PD)*	10-78	Need assistance
10-51	Wrecker needed	10-79	Notify coroner
10-52	Ambulance needed	10-80	Chase in progress
10-53	Road blocked at. . .	10-81	Breathalyzer report
10-54	Livestock on highway	10-82	Reserve lodging
10-55	Introxicated driver	10-83	Work school xing at. . .
10-56	Intoxicated pedestrian	10-84	If meeting. . . advise time
10-57	Hit and Run (F, PI, PD)*	10-85	Delayed due to. . .
10-58	Direct traffic	10-86	Officer/operator on duty
10-59	Convoy or escort	10-87	Pick up/distribute checks
10-60	Squad in vicinity		
10-61	Personnel in area		

* F, PI, and PD mean, respectively, Fatality, Personal Injury, and Property Damage.

10-88	Advise present telephone number of...	10-94	Drag racing
10-89	Bomb threat	10-95	Prisoner/suspect in custody
10-90	Bank alarm at...	10-96	Mental subject
10-91	Pick up prisoner/ suspect	10-97	Test signal
10-92	Improperly parked vehicle	10-98	Prison/jail break
10-93	Blockade	10-99	Records indicate wanted

Most newsrooms will be equipped with so-called "public service" radio receivers. These are the police, fire, and other emergency units communications systems. You will hear a great deal of useful information on them, but what you hear can be used only as a tip. You may not, under federal law, directly use any information you may gather in that manner. It is considered a serious offense and carries a heavy fine.

Patient Conditions

Patient conditions are defined by the American Hospital Association, and are recognized and followed by most hospitals.

Good—Vital signs are stable and within normal limits. Patient is conscious and comfortable; indicators are excellent.

Fair—Vital signs are stable and within normal limits. Patient is conscious but may be uncomfortable; indicators are favorable.

Serious—Vital signs may be unstable and not within normal limits. Patient is acutely ill; indicators are questionable.

Critical—Vital signs are unstable and not within normal limits. Patient may not be conscious; indicators are unfavorable.

A spokesman for the American Hospital Association told me "The use of the phrase 'in critical but stable condition' is, in my view, contradictory."

State Capitals

State	Capital
ALABAMA	MONTGOMERY
ALASKA	JUNEAU (JOO-noh)
ARIZONA	PHOENIX
ARKANSAS	LITTLE ROCK
CALIFORNIA	SACRAMENTO (Note spelling)
COLORADO	DENVER
CONNECTICUT	HARTFORD (HART-furd)
DELAWARE	DOVER
FLORIDA	TALLAHASSEE
GEORGIA	ATLANTA
HAWAII	HONOLULU
IDAHO	BOISE (BOY-zee)
ILLINOIS	SPRINGFIELD
INDIANA	INDIANAPOLIS
IOWA	DES MOINES (duh-MOYN)
KANSAS	TOPEKA
KENTUCKY	FRANKFORT (FRANK-furt)
LOUISIANA	BATON ROUGE (BAT-un ROOJH)
MAINE	AUGUSTA
MARYLAND	ANNAPOLIS
MASSACHUSETTS	BOSTON (BAW-stun)
MICHIGAN	LANSING
MINNESOTA	SAINT PAUL

State	Capital
MISSISSIPPI	JACKSON
MISSOURI	JEFFERSON CITY
MONTANA	HELENA (HELL-ih-nuh)
NEBRASKA	LINCOLN
NEVADA	CARSON CITY
NEW HAMPSHIRE	CONCORD (KAWN-kurd)
NEW JERSEY	TRENTON
NEW MEXICO	SANTA FE (SAN-tuh FAY)
NEW YORK	ALBANY
NORTH CAROLINA	RALEIGH
NORTH DAKOTA	BISMARCK
OHIO	COLUMBUS
OKLAHOMA	OKLAHOMA CITY
OREGON	SALEM
PENNSYLVANIA	HARRISBURG
RHODE ISLAND	PROVIDENCE
SOUTH CAROLINA	COLUMBIA
SOUTH DAKOTA	PIERRE (PEER)
TENNESSEE	NASHVILLE
TEXAS	AUSTIN
UTAH	SALT LAKE CITY
VERMONT	MONTPELIER (mawnt-PEEL-yur)
VIRGINIA	RICHMOND
WASHINGTON	OLYMPIA
WEST VIRGINIA	CHARLESTON
WISCONSIN	MADISON
WYOMING	CHEYENNE (shy-ANN)

Nations of the World and Capitals

In broadcast newswriting unfamiliar foreign city names are usually omitted and the location of an event is related to the nation's capital city (300 miles southeast of Manila, rather than 35 miles west of Iloilo City). It is hoped this list will provide a quick reference to the general location of foreign nations and the pronunciation of them and their capitals.

NATION	CAPITAL CITY
Afghanistan (S Central Asia)	Kabul (KUHB-uhl)
Albania (S Europe, Adriatic)	Tiranë (tih-RAHN-uh)
Algeria (NW Africa)	Algiers (al-JEERS)
Andorra (W Europe, S. France)	Andorra la Vella (an-DOR-uh luh-VAY-yuh)
Angola (SW Africa)	Luanda (loo-AN-duh)
Antigua and Barbuda (an-TEE-guh and bar-BOOD- uh) (E Caribbean)	Saint John
Argentina (S America)	Buenos Aires (BWAY-noh SAR-eez)
Australia (SE of Asia, S Pacific)	Canberra (KAN-buruh)
Austria (S Central Europe)	Vienna (vee-EHN-uh)

NATION	CAPITAL CITY
Bahama (Atlantic, E Florida)	Nassau (NAS-aw)
Bahrain (bah-RAYN) (Persian Gulf)	Manama (muh-NAM-uh)
Bangladesh (S Asia, E India)	Dacca (DAK-uh)
Barbados (bar-BAYD-ohs) (W Indies)	Bridgetown
Belgium (NW Europe)	Brussels (BRUHS-uhls)
Belize (buh-LEEZ) (Central America)	Belmopan (bel-moh-PAN)
Benin (buh-NIN) (West Africa)	Porto-Novo (POHRT-oh-NOH-voh)
Bhutan (boo-TAWN) (E Himalayas)	Thimbu (thihm-POO)
Bolivia (South America)	La Paz (administrative) (luh-PAHZ) Sucre (constitutional) (SOO-kruh)
Botswana (bawt-SWAHN-uh) (Southern Africa)	Gaborone (gab-uh-ROHN)
Brazil (South America)	Brasilia (bruh-ZEEL-yuh)
Brunei (broo-NYE) (Island of Borneo)	Bandar Seri Begawan (ban-dur sihr-ee buh-GAH-wun)
Bulgaria (E Europe—Balkan pen.)	Sofia (soh-FEE-uh or SOH-fee-uh)
Burma (S Asia, N Thailand)	Rangoon (ran-GOON)
Burundi (boo-ROON-dee) (Central Africa)	Bujuambura (BOO-juhm-BOOR-uh)
Cambodia (SE Asia)	Phnom Penh (puh-NOM PEHN)
Cameroun (West Central Africa)	Yaoundé (yawoon-DAY)

NATION	CAPITAL CITY
Canada (North America)	Ottawa (AWT-uh-wuh)
Provinces	
Alberta	Edmondton
British Columbia	Victoria
Manitoba	Winnipeg
New Brunswick	Fredericton
Newfoundland (Incl. Labrador)	Saint John's
Nova Scotia	Halifax
Ontario	Toronto
Prince Edward Island	Charlottetown
Quebec (kweh-BEHK)	Quebec City
Saskatchewan	Regina (ruh-JY-nuh)
Cape Verde (Atlantic islands, W Africa)	Praia (PRY-uh)
Central African Republic (Central Africa)	Bangui (BAWN-geh)
Chad (North Central Africa)	N'Djamena (Fort-Lamy) (ehn-JAWM-uh-nuh or FOR-luh-MEE)
Chile (South America)	Santiago (Sant-ee-ahg-oh)
China (Mainland), People's Republic of (Asia)	Peking or Beijing (PEE-KING) (BAY-ZHING)
China (Taiwan) (Asia)	Taipei (TY-PAY)
Colombia (NW South America)	Bogotá (boh-guh-TAW)
Comoro Islands (KAWM-eh-row) (E Africa)	Moroni (mah-ROH-nee)
Congo Republic (W Central Africa)	Brazzaville (BRAZ-uh-vihl)
Costa Rica (Central America)	San José (San-uh-ZAY)

NATION	CAPITAL CITY
Cuba (West Indies)	Havana (huh-VAN-uh)
Cyprus (E Mediterranean)	Nicosia (nihk-uh-SEE-uh)
Czechoslovakia (E Central Europe)	Prague (PRAHG)
Denmark (N Europe)	Copenhagen (koh-phn-HAY-guhn)
Djibouti (jih-BOOT-ee) (E Africa)	Jibuti
Dominica (dawm-ih-NEE-kuh or doh-MIHN-ih kuh) (E Caribbean)	Roseau (roh-ZOH)
Dominican Republic (West Indies, Hispanola)	Santo Domingo (sawn-uhd-uh-MINH-go)
Ecuador (South America)	Quito (KEE-toh)
Egypt (NE Africa)	Cairo (KY-roh)
El Salvador (Cental America)	San Salvador (sawn SAL-vuh-dohr)
Equatorial Guinea (GIHN-ee) (W Coast Africa)	Malabo (maw-LAW-boh)
Ethiopia (E Africa)	Addis Ababa (AWD-uh-SAWB-uh-buh)
Fiji (FEE-jee) (S Pacific)	Suva (SOO-vuh)
Finland (N Baltic Europe)	Helsinki (hehl-SIN-kee)
France (W Europe)	Paris (PAIR-us)
Gabon (guh-BAWN) (W Africa)	Libreville (LEE-bruh-VEL)
Gambia, The (GAM-bee-uh) (W Africa)	Banjul (BAWN-jool)
Germany, East (German Democratic Republic) (Central Europe)	East Berlin (buhr-LYN)

NATION	CAPITAL CITY
Germany, West (Federal Republic of Germany) (Central Europe)	Bonn (BAWN)
Ghana (SW Africa)	Accra (uh-KRAW)
Greece (SE Europe, Balkan pen.)	Athens (ATH-uhnz)
Grenada (gruh-NAYD-uh) (Caribbean, near Venezuela)	Saint George's
Guatemala (Central America)	Guatemala City (Gwawt-uh-MAWL-uh)
Guinea (GIHN-ee) (W Africa)	Conakry (KAWN-uh-kree)
Guinea-Bissau (bihs-OW) (W Africa)	Bissau (bis-OW)
Guyana (guy-AN-uh) (N South America)	Georgetown
Haiti (HAYT-ee) (Shares Hispaniola with Dominican Republic)	Port-au-Prince (POART-oh-PRINZ)
Honduras (hawn-DOOR-us) (Central America)	Tegucigalpa (tuh-goo-suh-GAL-puh)
Hungary (Central Europe)	Budapest (BOOD-uh-pehst)
Iceland (N Atlantic, Arctic)	Reykjavik (RAYK-yuh-vehk)
India (S Asia)	New Delhi (noo DEHL-ee)
Indonesia (ihn-doh-NEE-zjuh) (SE Asia)	Dakarta (juh-KART-uh)
Iran (I-RAWN) (Middle East, S. Asia)	Tehran (tay-uh-RAN)
Iraq (ih-RAK) (Middle East)	Baghdad (BAG-dad)
Ireland (W of Great Britain)	Dublin
Israel (IHZ-ree-ul) (E Mediterranean)	Jerusalem

NATION	CAPITAL CITY
Italy (S Europe, Mediterranean)	Rome
Ivory Coast (SW Africa)	Abidjan (ab-eh-jawn)
Jamaica (juh-MAY-kuh) (West Indies)	Kingston
Japan (E Asia)	Tokyo (TOH-kee-oh)
Jordan (W Asia)	Amman (uh-MAWN)
Kenya (KEHN-yuh or KEEN-yuh) (E Africa)	Nairobi (nye-ROH-bee)
Kiribati (KIR-uh-bas) (S Pacific islands)	Tarawa (Teh-RAW-wuh or TAR-uh-wuh)
Korea, North (NE Asia)	Pyongyang (pee-YUNG-yahn)
Korea, South (NE Asia)	Seoul (SOHL)
Kuwait (koo-WAYT) (SW Asia)	Kuwait City (koo-WAYT)
Laos (LAW-ohs) (SE Asia)	Vientiane (veey-EHN-tyawn)
Lebanon (SW Asia)	Beirut (bay-ROOT)
Lesotho (leh-SOH-too) (Surrounded by Republic of South Africa)	Maseru (MAZ-uh-roo)
Liberia (lye-BEER-ee-uh) (SW Africa)	Monrovia (muhn-ROH-vee-uh)
Libya (LIB-ee-uh) (N Africa)	Tripoli (THIHP-oh-lee)
Liechtenstein (LIHK-tuhn-SHTEYN) (W Europe, Alpine)	Vaduz (vah-DOOTZ)
Luxembourg (LUH-suhm-burg) (W Europe)	Luxembourg (LUHK-suhm-burg)

NATION	CAPITAL CITY
Madagascar (Indian Ocean, E Africa)	Antananarivo (an-tuh-nan-uh-REE-voh)
Malawi (mah-LAH-wee) (SE Africa)	Lilongwe (lee-LAWNG-way)
Malaysia (muh-LAYJ-zuh) (SE Asia and Borneo)	Kuala Lumpur (KWAWL-uh LOOM-poor)
Maldives (MAL-dyvz) (Islands Indian Ocean)	Male (MAHL-ee)
Mali (MAHL-ee) (W Africa)	Bamako (bam-uh-KOH)
Malta (Mediterranean)	Valletta (vuh-LET-uh)
Mauritania (W Africa)	Nouakchott (new-AWK-shawt)
Mauritius (maw-RISH-ee-uhs) (Indian Ocean, E Africa)	Port Louis (LOO-ihs or LOO-ee or loo-EE)
Mexico (S North America)	Mexico City
Monaco (MAWN-uh-koh) (S Europe)	Monaco
Mongolia (E Central Asia)	Ulan Bator (oo-lawn-BAW-tor)
Morocco (NW Africa)	Rabat (ruh-BAWT)
Mozambique (moh-zam-BEEK) (SE Africa)	Maputo (mah-POO-toh)
Nauru (naw-OO-roo) (S Pacific)	Yaren (YAHR-ruhn)
Nepal(nuh-PAWL) (Himalayas)	Kathmandu (kat-man-DOO)
Netherlands (Holland) (NW Europe)	Amsterdam
New Zealand (S Pacific)	Wellington
Nicaragua (NIHK-uh-RAWG-wuh) (Central America)	Managua (muh-NAWG-wuh)

NATION	CAPITAL CITY
Niger (NY-juhr) (W Africa)	Niamey (nee-AWM-ay)
Nigeria (ny-JEER-ee-uh) (W Africa)	Lagos (LAY-gaws)
Norway (NW Europe)	Oslo
Oman (oh-MAWN) (SW Asia)	Muscat (MUHS-kat)
Pakistan (S Asia)	Islamabad (ihz-LAWM-uh-bawd)
Panama (Central America)	Panama City
Papua New Guinea (S Pacific, N Australia) (Shares island with Indonesia)	Port Moresby
Paraguay (South America)	Asunción (ah-soon-see-OHN)
Peru (South America)	Lima (LEE-muh)
Philippines (Islands off E Asia)	Manila (muh-NIHL-uh)
Poland (E Europe)	Warsaw
Portugal (SW Europe)	Lisbon (LIHZ-buhn)
Qatar (KAWT-uhr) (W Persian Gulf)	Doha (DOO-hah)
Romania (SE Europe)	Bucharest (BOO-kuh-rehst)
Rwanda (ru-AWN-duh) (E Central Africa)	Kigali (kih-GAWL-ee)
Saint Kitts-Nevis (E. Caribbean)	Basseterre (baws-TAHR)
Saint Lucia (LOO-shuh) (E Caribbean)	Castries (KAS-treez)
Saint Vincent and the Grenadines (E Caribbean)	Kingstown

NATION	CAPITAL CITY
San Marino (SAN muh-REE-noh) (Surrounded by Italy)	San Marino (san muh-REE-noh)
Sao Tome and Principe (sount-uh-mee and PREEN-see-pih) (Atlantic Islands off Central Africa)	Sao Tome
Saudi Arabia (SAWD-ee) (Arabian Pen. Middle East)	Riyadh (ree-YAWD)
Senegal (sehn-eh-GAWL) (W Africa)	Dakar (DAK-ahr)
Seychelles (say-SHELL) (Indian Ocean island group)	Victoria
Sierra Leone (see-AIR-uh lee-OHN) (W Africa)	Freetown
Singapore (Island off S Ma lay Pen.)	Singapore (SIN-guh-pohr)
Solomon Islands (W Pacific)	Honiara (hoh-nee-AWR-uh)
Somalia (so-MAWL-ee-uh) (E Africa)	Mogadishu (MAWG-uh-DISH-oo)
South Africa, Republic of (S Africa)	Cape Town (legislative) Pretoria (administrative)
Spain (SW Europe)	Madrid (muh-DRIHD)
Sri Lanka (shree-LAWN-kuh) (SE India)	Colombo (kuh-LUHM-boh)
Sudan (soo-DAN) (Eastern Sahara)	Khartoum (kahr-TOOM)
Suriname (suhr-ih-NAWM-ih) (N South America)	Paramaribo (PAR-eh-MAHR-ih-boh)
Swaziland (SWAHZ-ee-land) (S Africa)	Mbabane (ehm-bah-BAHN)
Sweden (N Europe)	Stockholm

NATION	CAPITAL CITY
Switzerland (Europe, Alpine)	Bern (BURN)
Syria (SW Asia)	Damascus (duh-MAS-kuhs)
Tanzania (tan-zuh-NEE-uh) (E Africa)	Dar-es-Salaam (dahr-ehs-suh-LAWM)
Thailand (TYE-land) (SE Asia)	Bangkok (BANG-kawk)
Togo (W Africa)	Lomé (loh-MAY)
Tonga (S Pacific)	Nukualofa (NOO-koo-eh-LOH-fuh)
Trinidad and Tobago (tuh-BAY-goh) (S Atlantic off Venzuela)	Port of Spain
Tunisia (too-NEE-zee-uh) (N Africa)	Tunis (TOO-Nihs)
Turkey (Asia Minor, Mediterranean)	Ankara (ANG-kuh-ruh)
Tuvalu (too-VAHL-oo) (SW Pacific)	Funafuti (foo-nah-FOOT-ee)
Uganda (yoo-GAN-duh) (E Africa)	Kampala (kahm-PAHL-uh)
Union of Soviet Socialist Republics (Commonly called Russia) (N Asia)	Moscow (MAWS-kow or MAWS-koh)
United Arab Emirates (Seven Arab Countries) (Persian Gulf)	Abu Dhabi (awb-oo-THAWB-ee)
United Kingdom (England, Scotland, Wales, and N Ireland) (NW Europe)	London
United States of America (North America)	Washington, D.C.

NATION	CAPITAL CITY
Upper Volta (nowknown as Burkina Faso) (W Africa)	Ouagadougou (waug-uh-DOO-goo)
Uruguay (South America)	Montevideo mawnt-uh-vih-DAY-oh
Vanuatu (van-uh-WAHT-oo) (SW Pacific)	Vila (VEE-luh)
Vatican City (Roman Catholic city-state) (Within Rome, Italy)	
Venezuela (Vehn-ehz-WAY-luh) (South America)	Caracas (kuh-RAWK-uhs)
Vietnam (vee-EHT NAWM) (SE Asia)	Hanoi (haw-NOY)
Western Samoa (suh-MOH-uh) (S Pacific)	Apia (ah-PEE-uh)
Yemen, Northern (YEM-uhn) (Arabian pen.)	Sana (SAN-aw)
Yemen, Southern (Arabian pen.)	Aden (AWD-n)
Yugoslavia (SE Europe)	Belgrade (BEHL-grayd)
Zaire (ZYE-eer or za-IR) (Central Africa)	Kinshasa (kihn-SHAWS-uh)
Zambia (ZAM-bee-uh) (S Central Africa)	Lusaka (loo-SAWK-uh)
Zimbabwe (zihm-BAWB-way) (S Africa)	Harare (huh-RAW-ray)

Area Codes

By state with Time Zone

Atlantic Time (AT) = New York plus one hour
Eastern Time (ET) = New York
Central Time (CT) = New York minus one hour
Mountain time (MT) = New York minus two hours
Pacific Time (PT) = New York minus three hours
Alaska Time (AT) = New York minus four hours
Hawaii Time (HT) = New York minus five hours

STATE CITY	AREA CODE	TIME ZONE
Alabama	205	(CT)
Alaska	907	(AT)
Arizona	602	(MT)
Arkansas	501	(CT)
California		(PT)
Bakersfield	805	
Fresno	209	
Los Angeles	213 and 818	
Orange	714	
Sacramento	916	
San Diego	619	
San Francisco	415	
San Jose	408	
Santa Rosa	707	
Colorado	303	(MT)

STATE CITY	AREA CODE	TIME ZONE
Connecticut	203	(ET)
Delaware	302	(ET)
District of Columbia (Washington, DC)	202	(ET)
Florida		(ET)
Ft. Lauderdale	305	
Ft. Myers	813	
Jacksonville	904	
Miami	305	
Georgia		(ET)
Atlanta	404	
Waycross	912	
Hawaii	808	(HT)
Idaho	208	(MT)
Illinois		(CT)
Chicago	312	
Mt. Vernon	618	
Peoria	309	
Rockford	815	
Springfield	217	
Indiana		(ET)
Evansville	812	
Indianapolis	317	
South Bend	219	
Iowa		(CT)
Council Bluffs	712	
Des Moines	515	
Dubuque	319	
Kansas		(CT, except MT West)
Topeka	913	
Wichita	316	
Kentucky		(ET East, CT West)
Covington	606	
Louisville	502	

STATE CITY	AREA CODE	TIME ZONE
Louisiana		(CT)
Lake Charles	318	
New Orleans	504	
Maine	207	(ET)
Maryland	301	(ET)
Massachusetts		(ET)
Boston	617	
Springfield	413	
Michigan		(ET)
Battle Creek	616	
Detroit	313	
Escanaba	906	
Saginaw	517	
Minnesota		(CT)
Duluth	218	
Minneapolis	612	
Rochester	507	
Mississippi	601	(CT)
Missouri		(CT)
Joplin	417	
Kansas Cith	816	
St. Louis	314	
Montana	406	(MT, exept for PT West)
Nebraska		(CT East, MT West)
North Platte	308	
Omaha	402	
Nevada	702	(PT)
New Hampshire	603	(ET)
New Jersey		(ET)
Atlantic City	609	
Newark	201	
New Mexico	505	(MT)

STATE CITY	AREA CODE	TIME ZONE
New York		(ET)
Albany	518	
Brooklyn	718	
Buffalo	716	
Elmira	607	
Hempstead	516	
Manhattan	212	
Syracuse	315	
White Plains	914	
North Carolina		(ET)
Charlotte	704	
Winston-Salem	919	
North Dakota	701	(CT East and North, MT Southwest)
Ohio		(ET)
Cincinnati	513	
Cleveland	216	
Columbus	614	
Toledo	419	
Oklahoma		(CT)
Oklahoma City	405	
Tulsa	918	
Oregon	503	(PT; except for MT Southeast corner)
Pennsylvania		(ET)
Erie	814	
Harrisburg	717	
Philadelphia	215	
Pittsburgh	412	
Puerto Rico	809	(AT)
Rhode Island	401	(ET)
South Carolina	803	(ET)
South Dakota	605	(CT East, MT West)
Tennessee		(ET East, CT West)
Memphis	901	
Nashville	615	

STATE CITY	AREA CODE	TIME ZONE
Texas		(CT, except for MT Southwest corner)
Amarillo	806	
Austin	512	
Dallas	214	
Galveston	409	
Houston	713	
Sweetwater	915	
Temple	817	
Utah	801	(MT)
Vermont	802	(ET)
Virginia		(ET)
Richmond	804	
Roanoke	703	
Virgin Islands	809	(AT)
Washington		(PT)
Seattle	206	
Walla Walla	509	
West Virginia	304	(ET)
Wisconsin		(CT)
Eau Claire	715	
Madison	608	
Milwaukee	414	
Wyoming	307	(MT)
Canada		
Alberta	403	(MT)
Brit. Columbia	604	(PT)
Manitoba	204	(CT)
New Brunswick	506	(AT)
Newfoundland	709	(AT)
Northwest Terr	403	
Nova Scotia	902	(AT)
Ontario		(ET East, CT West)
London	519	
North	705	

STATE CITY	AREA CODE	TIME ZONE
Ottawa	613	
Thunder Bay	807	
Toronto	416	
Pr. Edward Is.	902	(AT)
Quebec		(ET)
Montreal	514	
Quebec City	418	
Sherbrooke	819	
Saskatchewan	306	(CT East and North, MT Northwest)
Yukon	403	(MT East, PT West)
Northwest Territories	403	(MT East, PT West)

By Number

201	New Jersey		304	West Virginia
202	Washington, DC		305	Florida
203	Connecticut		306	Saskatchewan
204	Manitoba		307	Wyoming
205	Alabama		308	Nebraska
206	Washington State		309	Illinois
207	Maine		312	Illinois
208	Idaho		313	Michigan
209	California		314	Missouri
212	New York		315	New York
213	California		316	Kansas
214	Texas		317	Indiana
215	Pennsylvania		318	Louisiana
216	Ohio		319	Iowa
217	Illinois		401	Rhode Island
218	Minnesota		402	Nebraska
219	Indiana		403	Alberta, Northwest Territories, Yukon
301	Maryland			
302	Delaware		404	Georgia
303	Colorado		405	Oklahoma

406	Montana	609	New Jersey
408	California	612	Minnesota
409	Texas	613	Ontario
412	Pennsylvania	614	Ohio
413	Massachusetts	615	Tennessee
414	Wisconsin	616	Michigan
415	California	617	Massachusetts
416	Ontario	618	Illinois
417	Missouri	619	California
418	Quebec	701	North Dakota
419	Ohio	702	Nevada
501	Arkansas	703	Virginia
502	Kentucky	704	North Carolina
503	Oregon	705	Ontario
504	Louisiana	707	California
505	New Mexico	709	Newfoundland
506	New Brunswick	712	Iowa
507	Minnesota	713	Texas
509	Washington State	714	California
512	Texas	715	Wisconsin
513	Ohio	716	New York
514	Quebec	717	Pennsylvania
515	Iowa	718	New York
516	New York	800	Inward WATS
517	Michigan	801	Utah
518	New York	802	Vermont
519	Ontario	803	South Carolina
601	Mississippi	804	Virginia
602	Arizona	805	California
603	New Hampshire	806	Texas
604	British Columbia	807	Ontario
605	South Dakota	808	Hawaii
606	Kentucky	809	Bahamas, Puerto Rico, Virgin Islands
607	New York		
608	Wisconsin	812	Indiana

813	Florida	904	Florida
814	Pennsylvania	906	Michigan
815	Illinois	907	Alaska
816	Missouri	912	Georgia
817	Texas	913	Kansas
818	California	914	New York
819	Quebec	915	Texas
901	Tennessee	916	California
902	Nova Scotia, Prince Edward Island	918	Oklahoma
		919	North Carolina

International Dialing Codes

For foreign calls: 011-(country code)-(city code, if any)-number.

Algeria*	213	Denmark	45
American Samoa*	684	Ecuador	593
Andorra	33	Egypt	20
Argentina	54	El Salvador*	503
Australia	61	Ethiopia	251
Austria	43	Fiji*	679
Bahrain*	973	Finland	358
Belgium	32	France	33
Belize	501	French Antilles*	596
Bolivia	591	Gabon*	241
Brazil	55	German Dem. Rep.	37
Cameroon*	237	German Fed. Rep.	49
Chile	56	Greece	30
China (Taiwan)	886	Guam*	671
Colombia	57	Guatemala	502
Costa Rica*	506	Guyana	592
Cyprus	357	Haiti	509
Czechoslovakia	42	Honduras*	504

* No city code needed. City codes and additional country codes available from local operators.

Hong Kong	852	Pakistan	92
Hungary	36	Panama*	507
Iceland	354	Papua New Guinea*	675
India	91	Paraguay	595
Indonesia	62	Peru	51
Iran	98	Philippines	63
Iraq	964	Poland	48
Ireland, Rep. of	353	Portugal	351
Israel	972	Qatar*	974
Italy	39	Romania	40
Ivory Coast*	225	Saipan*	670
Japan	81	San Marino	39
Jordan	962	Saudi Arabia	966
Kenya	254	Senegal*	221
Korea, Rep. of	82	Singapore*	65
Kuwait*	965	South Africa	27
Liberia*	231	Spain	34
Libya	218	Sri Lanka	94
Liechtenstein	41	Suriname*	597
Luxembourg*	352	Sweden	46
Malawi	265	Switzerland	41
Malaysia	60	Tahiti*	689
Mexico	52	Thailand	66
Monaco	33	Tunisia	216
Morocco	212	Turkey	90
Nzmibiz	264	United Arab	
Nertherlands	31	Emirates	971
Netherlands		United Kingdom	44
Antilles	599	Uruguay	598
New Caledonia	687	Vatican City	39
New Zealand	64	Venezuela	58
Nicaragua	505	Yemen Arab	
Nigeria	234	Republic	967
Norway	47	Yugoslavia	38
Oman*	968		

Codes of Ethics

Radio-Television News Directors Association*

The members of the Radio-Television News Directors Association agree that their prime responsibility as journalists—and that of the broadcasting industry as the collective sponsor of news broadcasting—is to provide to the public they serve a news service as accurate, full and prompt as human integrity and devotion can devise. To that end, they declare their acceptance of the standards of practice here set forth, and their solemn intent to honor them to the limits of their ability.

Article One

> The primary purpose of broadcast journalists—to inform the public of events of importance and appropriate interest in a manner that is accurate and comprehensive —shall override all other purposes.

Article Two

> Broadcast news presentations shall be designed not only to offer timely and accurate information, but also to present it in the light of relevant circumstances that give it meaning and perspective.
> This standard means that news reports, when clarity demands it, will be laid against pertinent factual background; that factors such as race, creed, nationality, or prior status will be reported only when they are relevant;

---

* Reprinted with permission of Radio-Television News Directors Association, Washington, D.C.

that comment or subjective content will be properly identified; and that errors in fact will be promptly acknowledged and corrected.

Article Three

Broadcast journalists shall seek to select material for news-casts solely on their evaluation of its merits as news.

This standard means that news will be selected on the criteria of significance, community and regional relevance, appropriate human interest, service to defined audiences. It excludes sensationalism or misleading emphasis in any form; subservience to external or "interested" efforts to influence news selection and presentation, whether from within the broadcasting industry or from without. It requires that such terms as "bulletin" and "flash" can be used only when the character of the news justifies them; that bombastic or misleading descriptions of newsroom facilities and personnel be rejected, along with undue use of sound and visual effects; and that promotional or publicity material be sharply scrutinized before use and identified by source or otherwise when broadcast.

Article Four

Broadcast journalists shall at all times display humane respect for the dignity, privacy and well-being of persons with whom the news deals.

Article Five

Broadcast journalists shall govern their personal lives and such non-professional associations as may impinge on their professional activities in a manner that will protect them from conflict of interest, real or apparent.

Article Six

Broadcast journalists shall seek actively to present all news, the knowledge of which will serve the public interest, no matter what selfish, uninformed or corrupt efforts attempt to color it, withhold it or prevent its presentation. They shall make constant efforts to open doors closed to the reporting of public proceedings with tools appropriate to broadcasting (including cameras and recorders), consistent with the public interest. They acknowledge the journalist's ethic of protection of confidential information and sources and urge unswerving observation of it except in instances in which it would clearly and unmistakably defy the public interest.

Article Seven

Broadcast journalists recognize the responsibility borne by broadcasting for informed analysis, comment and editorial opinion on public events and issues. They accept the obligation of broadcasters for the presentation of such matters by individuals whose competence, experience and judgment qualify them for it.

Article Eight

In court, broadcast journalists shall conduct themselves with dignity, whether the court is in or out of session. They shall keep broadcast equipment as unobtrusive and silent as possible. Where court facilities are inadequate, pool broadcasts should be arranged.

Article Nine

In reporting matters that are or may be litigated, the journalist shall avoid practices which would tend to interfere with the right of an individual to a fair trial.

Article Ten

Broadcast journalists shall not misrepresent the source of any broadcast news material.

Article Eleven

Broadcast journalists shall actively censure and seek to prevent violations of these standards, and shall actively encourage their observance by all journalists, whether of the Radio-Television News Directors Association or not.

*Society of Professional Journalists/Sigma Delta Chi**

The Society of Professional Journalists, Sigma Delta Chi, believes the duty of journalists is to serve the truth.

We believe the agencies of mass communication are carriers of public discussion and information, acting on their Constitutional mandate and freedom to learn and report the facts.

We believe in public enlightenment as the forerunner of justice, and in our Constitutional role to seek the truth as part of the public's right to know the truth.

We believe those responsibilities carry obligations that require journalists to perform with intelligence, objectivity, accuracy, and fairness.

To these ends, we declare acceptance of the standards of practice here set forth:

Responsibility

The public's right to know of events of public importance and interest is the overriding mission of the mass media. The purpose of distributing news and enlightened opinion is to serve the general welfare. Journalists who use their professional status as representatives of the public for selfish or other unworthy motives violate a high trust.

Freedom of the Press

Freedom of the press is to be guarded as an inalienable right of people in a free society. It carries with it the freedom and responsibility to discuss, question, and challenge actions and utterances of our government and of our public and private institutions. Journalists uphold the right to speak unpopular opinions and the privilege to agree with the majority.

Ethics

Journalists must be free of obligation to any interest other than the public's right to know the truth.

1. Gifts, favors, free travel, special treatment, or pri-

* Reprinted with permission of Society of Professional Journalists/Sigma delta Chi, Chicago.

vileges can compromise the integrity of journalists and their employers. Nothing of value should be accepted.

2. Secondary employment, political involvement, holding public office, and service in community organizations should be avoided if it compromises the integrity of journalists and their employers. Journalists and their employers should conduct their personal lives in a manner which protects them from conflict of interest, real or apparent. Their responsibilities to the public are paramount. That is the nature of their profession.

3. So-called news communications from private sources should not be published or broadcast without substantiation of their claims to news value.

4. Journalists will seek news that serves the public interest, despite the obstacles. They will make constant efforts to assure that the public's business is conducted in public and that public records are open to public inspection.

5. Journalists acknowledge the newsman's ethic of protecting confidential sources of information.

Accuracy and Objectivity

Good faith with the public is the foundation of all worthy journalism.

1. Truth is our ultimate goal.

2. Objectivity in reporting the news is another goal, which serves as the mark of an experienced professional. It is a standard of performance toward which we strive. We honor those who achieve it.

3. There is no excuse for inaccuracies or lack of thoroughness.

4. Newspaper headlines should be fully warranted by the contents of the articles they accompany. Photographs and telecasts should give an accurate picture of an event and not highlight a minor incident out of context.

5. Sound practice makes clear distinction between news reports and expressions of opinion. News reports should be free of opinion or bias and represent all sides of an issue.

6. Partisanship in editorial comment which knowingly departs from the truth violates the spirit of American journalism.

7. Journalists recognize their responsibility for offering informed analysis, comment, and editorial opinion on public events and issues. They accept the obligation to present such material by individuals whose competence, experience, and judgment qualify them for it.
8. Special articles or presentations devoted to advocacy or the writer's own conclusions and interpretations should be labeled as such.

Fair Play

Journalists at all times will show respect for the dignity, privacy, rights, and well-being of people encountered in the course of gathering and presenting the news.

1. The news media should not communicate unofficial charges affecting reputation or moral character without giving the accused a chance to reply.
2. The news media must guard against invading a person's right to privacy.
3. The media should not pander to morbid curiosity about details of vice and crime.
4. It is the duty of news media to make prompt and complete correction of their errors.
5. Journalists should be accountable to the public for their reports and the public should be encouraged to voice its grievances against the media. Open dialogue with our readers, viewers, and listeners should be fostered.

Pledge

Journalists should actively censure and try to prevent violations of these standards, and they should encourage their observance by all newspeople. Adherence to this code of ethics is intended to preserve the bond of mutual trust and respect between American journalists and the American People.

The FCC and the News

I preface this section with a caution: I am not a lawyer. What I present here is my understanding of some of the law of broadcasting that weighs on the news department and individual broadcast journalists. Your news department should have, at the very least, a company lawyer on retainer who is familiar with communication law. This section is intended to raise your consciousness about legal problems that might arise. It is not intended as a field guide to safe and happy broadcasting.

The Federal Communications Commission has very little in its rules, regulations and policies impinging directly on the content of news programs because the First Amendment says government may not get involved in such things. But, there are some areas where the FCC's rules, regulations and policies do seem to violate the First Amendment's intent. Such things as reporting illegal lottery information, and the use of indecent, profane or obscene language, are prohibited. On the other hand, the Fairness Doctrine and the political access rules (Section 315) as well as other rules and regulations, require that broadcasters put things on the air they may not wish to. That, too, is seen by some to be an infringement of the broadcast journalist's Constitutional protection from government interference.

It is a fact that the U.S. Supreme Court has opined that broadcasting does not enjoy the full protection of the First Amendment as does the printed press, because it is so pervasive.* That argument is not accepted by many broadcast journalists. The Radio-Television News Directors Association and other

---

* *Red Lion Broadcasting Co.* v. *FCC, United States* v. *Radio-Television News Directors Association*, 395 U.S. 367, S.CT. 1794, 23 L. Ed 2d 371 (1969).

groups are waging a continuing battle to establish parity with the print media.

Until that takes place, however, the broadcaster must adhere to the FCC's *rules and regs*, as they are known. For the front office in a broadcasting station, the ever-changing FCC directives can be maddening. For the newsroom, it's not quite such a burden. The present atmosphere favoring deregulation may someday see the abolition of the Fairness Doctrine and the political equal-time rules. For the moment, however, they are still concerns of the news department as well as other parts of a broadcast station. The news operation also plays a major role in the station's *promise versus performance equation.*

Promise Versus Performance

Broadcasting stations must file with the FCC on a regular basis statements indicating community problems the station has identified and what it intends to do about them through its programming. The news department, wearing its public affairs hat, will often get involved in that process. The *performance* may take the form of a series of feature stories, a documentary or other special programming to address community problems. How well a station follows through on its promise of meeting community needs is taken into account at license renewal time.

Section 315

Section 315 of the Federal Communications Act of 1934, as amended, contains the political equal time rules. Stated very simply, the rules say that when a broadcaster provides air time, free or paid for, to one candidate for a given public office, equal time must be made available to all other candidates for that same office. Bona fide news stories and events are exempt from the rule, as are documentaries where the candidate's appearance is incidental to the content of the documentary. A broadcaster may, in the case of local and state elections, decide not to provide time to any candidate. But, in the case of federal elections, which include elections for Congress, the broadcaster must provide time if the candidates request it, and must provide that time at the lowest possible cost on the rate card.

The broadcast journalist in day-to-day reporting on politicians will worry very little about Section 315. He or she will, however, be aware of balance in coverage of rival candidates.

The Fairness Doctrine

While Section 315 deals with people—political candidates—the Fairness Doctrine deals with issues, specifically controversial issues. It is intended to ensure that "controversial issues of public importance" are addressed fairly by broadcasters. It says—again to be very simple about it—that whenever a broadcaster allows one side of a controversial issue of public importance to be aired, he has a positive obligation to seek out responsible spokesmen for all other sides of that issue and provide them with equivalent opportunity. (Notice the difference between "equal time" and "equivalent opportunity.")

Personal Attack Rule

Within the Fairness Doctrine there is also a "personal attack rule" which provides reply opportunity for a person who may have been attacked on the air—but it must have been an attack within the context of a controversial issue of public importance. To say John Jones is a jerk, is not, in the meaning of the Personal Attack rule, a personal attack. However, to say John Jones is a jerk because he does not believe in the death penalty, does count as a personal attack. And, when such an attack does take place on your station, the station must make time available to Jones to reply, if he wants to.

Editorial Endorsements of Candidates

Finally, the Fairness Doctrine also includes provisions for reply when a broadcaster editorially endorses or comes out opposed to a candidate for public office. Here is the gray area where the Fairness Doctrince and Section 315 seem to overlap. Notice, here, that the reply is to a statement by the broadcaster, while under Section 315, the reply is to a statement by a rival candidate.

The preceding discussions of Section 315 and the Fairness Doctrine are bare bones. These can be very complicated issues and you should find more thorough treatment of them in basic texts on broadcast newswriting, telecommunications or communications law.

Rebroadcasting Signals

Generally, it is a violation of the law to rebroadcast an intercepted radio signal, such as police dispatchers talking to vehicles. Such intercepted information may be used as tips for news coverage, but may not be used as a primary source of news. There is an exception to the prohibition against using intercepted radio signals. In emergency situations, radio messages sent by amateur (ham) radio operators may be used by news broadcasters—either directly, on tape, or the information used to develop a story. You must use caution. Many times the hams will be relaying information they have received from someone else. There is no assurance their information is correct, not exaggerated or timely. Many hams are organized into one of several groups trained to handle emergency "traffic" in and out of areas where normal means of communications are disrupted. Their reports are generally accurate, timely and reliable. Hams, you should know, are also licensed by the FCC after a difficult examination. There's a good chance one or more of your station's engineers will be licensed hams. They can give you a great deal of information. Citizen Band (CB) operators are not required to take examinations nor to be truly "licensed." There is some question as to the legality of using intercepted CB signals. I would avoid using them.

Taping Telephone Interviews

Many radio reporters rely very heavily on their telephones both for routine reporting and for getting interviews. It is perfectly all right to tape record a telephone interview IF you have first obtained the permission of the subject. The best way to do that is to make the call with the tape recorder running, and ask if it's all right to tape the conversation for possible use on the air. If the subject agrees, you have that agreement on tape. If he or she disagrees, stop the tape and continue with taking notes. Telephone taping laws vary from state to state. In some states, all parties to a taping must, by law, know what's going on. In other states, only one party needs to be aware that a tape is being made. Those laws are intended to prevent illegal wire taps, but they also apply to all taping.

Obscenity, Indecency, Profanity

Social values change rapidly, and this is one area where change is very apparent. I don't think I've ever heard what would be considered a true obscenity deliberately uttered in a news program. But, what many people think of as profanities are being allowed to air daily. These are usually uttered by interview subjects or people making statements, but there have been cases where correspondents—that is, professional, trained broadcasters—have been heard to spill some pretty rotten stuff on the air. My personal beliefs go back to my training in early 1950s radio where *darn* was forbidden and where we were not permitted to play an instrumental version of a record the vocal version of which contained questionable lyrics. I still have trouble with deliberately airing profanity. Just call me old-fashioned.

Lotteries

Comes now a complicated issue. A lottery is illegal unless sponsored by a state or is somehow exempt. A broadcaster is not permitted by law to knowingly promote any criminal act. So, it is illegal to promote a lottery. EXCEPT: where the station is located in a state that has its own legal lottery. Then the station may broadcast advertisements, information, and winning ticket numbers for its home-state lottery. Stations in adjacent states may also broadcast that information, even though they may be licensed to another state. It is unclear whether the state-of-license must also conduct a lottery. The wording of the law is ambiguous on that point. If, however, your state does not have a legal lottery, nor does an adjacent state, you will be in violation of federal law, and probably your own state law, to in any way promote a lottery, no matter how worthy the organization conducting it. As a journalist, you might get caught on this one by running a feature story on a church conducting a lottery.

So, how do you know when a lottery is a lottery and not just an innocent contest? There are three elements which must be present to constitute a lottery: consideration, chance and prize. That sounds pretty simple, but it can get messy. *Consideration* is anything a person must pay or do to enter the lottery. Simply being present usually does not constitute consideration, unless the admission price was uncommonly high. Definitions of consideration vary from state to state. If in doubt, check with your local counsel. *Chance* is self-explanatory—there must be an element of chance in awarding of the prize. And, the *prize* is similarly not troublesome. There must be a prize or there's no lottery.

Emergency Announcements

The station's programming people and engineers need to be concerned about compliance with the Emergency Broadcast System (EBS) requirements. Those requirements include visual (in TV) captioning of the EBS message for the hearing-impaired. I believe it's a good idea for the news department to also provide visual captioning for any important announcement. You can imagine the fear that would be struck into the hearts of the deaf to see something on the screen that read: "WEATHER ALERT" and not have any idea what was going on. Most TV stations today have some sort of character generator that can be quickly used to create a written message to air along with the aural announcement. It's a rare emergency announcement that cannot wait two minutes to be captioned before airing. There's one more requirement related to this. TV stations broadcasting primarily in a foreign language, must caption emergency messages in both English and the foreign language.

Libel and Privacy

In areas of law directly affecting the journalist and his or her work, the laws of libel and privacy are the most likely to change over the next few years. It seems nearly every major case that comes before the U.S. Supreme Court makes some change in the interpretation of the laws of libel. Currently, *New York Times* v. *Sullivan** of 1964 still sets the guiding principle of "actual malice." However, any time a test of that principle comes before the courts, there is a chance it could be changed to the detriment of journalism.

The following is derived from *The Associated Press Stylebook and Libel Manual*, which outlines the current state of affairs in the field of libel law. As a working journalist, you must make it your business to keep up with court decisions and adjust your practices accordingly.

There is no sure way to avoid litigation for libel. The best way to protect yourself is to practice fair and accurate journalism. Libel actions are very often more troublesome than serious. Many actions are brought as "nuisance suits," which can be costly, but not very damaging. By far the largest number of suits are won by the plaintiff at the lower court level, but over-turned on appeal. Nonetheless, legal fees and other costs in a libel defense can be enormous. It is far best to avoid action where you can.

It is believed that many libel actions can be stopped early in the complaint simply by talking to the person who believes he or she has been defamed. It has been the traditional response in most newsrooms to take the "We stand by our story" approach.

* *New York Times Co.* v. *Sullivan*, 376 U.S. 254, 84 S.CT. 710, 11 L.Ed 2d 686 (1964).

That may be the "professional" or "tough guy" stance so lovingly nurtured by certain journalists since the days of *The Front Page**, but it come across to the public—especially a member of the public who believes him or herself to have been harmed by a journalist—as pure arrogance. Many a libel action can be turned aside by simply talking with the complainant, explaining how journalistic decisions are made and why. There seems to be some evidence that people feel impotent when faced by the media. Libel actions are brought as a means of getting the media's attention. A simple conversation in a sympathetic frame of mind can, it is believed, prevent a lot of expensive grief.

Not all cases, of course, can be turned aside so easily. Some, we must admit, are legitimate. That is what we will examine here.

Libel

The kind of story that is likely to generate a libel action is not the great big story involving great big people. Those kinds of stories usually deal with events and people that fall outside the realm of libel action: public figures, members of Congress, and so on. The stories that generate libel actions are the simple-minded things we deal with every day. They are the wedding stories, the engagement announcements, the auto wrecks. The little stories that affect only a very few people, but put those people in compromising or embarrassing light. The best protection is careful journalism. A phoned-in engagement announcement can be a practical joke, but a terribly embarrassing one for the victim. Everything should be checked out. It is not enough that you acted in good faith with no malicious intent. If you fail to practice careful journalism, you are very likely to get stung in a libel action.

Errors in facts, imprecise language, failure to double check can be disastrous.

For example, in a group arrest such as a drug bust, it's very unlikely that all those taken into custody will be facing identical charges. Some will be charged with possession with intent to

---

* The *Front Page*, a play first staged in 1928, set a stereotype of journalists by depicting a tough, hard-drinking reporter who would stop at nothing for a story. A comedy, it was taken seriously. The story has since been made into at least three motion pictures.

distribute, others only with possession, others only with possession of a "personal" amount and so on. It is actionable to publish an erroneous charge. There is no better protection than accuracy.

Accurate reporting is not always enough. Reporting the exact words of a person who is libeling someone else is actionable unless there is "privilege." Privilege applies to the speaker and means that whatever is said, no matter how awful, may be published with impunity. Privilege is invoked in a fair and impartial report of a legislative, judicial or other public and official proceeding. However, you must know what constitutes a "public proceeding" in your state. In some states, for example, it is not privileged to report on the filing of a summons before there has been any judicial action.

Police and court stories are frequent sources of libel actions. Many of them arise from reporting on an arrest before any charge has been made. Whenever accusations are made against a person, it is very wise to get balancing comment either from the accused or from some other person. It is also prudent to fully identify the accuser.

Simply put, libel is defamation—injury to reputation or character. Anything—words, pictures, even cartoons—that subject a person to public ridicule, hatred, shame, embarrassment or create a negative opinion of a person, are libels. Also libelous are stories that may be financially damaging to the subject.

There is only one sure defense against libel and that is if the facts of the story are provably true. The operative word here is *provably*. You must be able to go into a court and persuade the jury that what you published was the actual truth and that you can prove it.

Another defense, although less comforting, is privilege. Absolute privilege means that utterances by certain persons cannot be held to be libelous. As stated above, that applies to legislative debate, court testimony, public and official proceedings, such as City Council meetings. And, by extension, if the person making such utterances cannot be found guilty of libel, then the publication of such utterances cannot be found to be libelous either. Do not be misled. It is the circumstance of the utterance, not the person that's doing the uttering that's important. Members of Congress are absolutely privileged speaking on the floor of the House. Speaking in their offices, however, they are not. A lawyer cannot be sued for libel for what he or she says in the course of a trial, but what is said on the court house steps is not protected by privilege. And, neither is the publication of what is said.

The concept of "privilege" is based on the assumption that only through free, open and robust debate can the truth or the wisest course of action be determined. It is the same basis—from John Milton—that gives us the concept of freedom of speech and press. To the extent that society needs to hear legislative, judicial and public discussions the rights of the individual who may be damaged are subordinated to the public interest.

As long as the reporting of privileged material is accurate and fair and free of malice, libel action cannot be brought for the publication of such material. The privilege of the press is considered to be "qualified," not absolute. It is qualified by the requirement that the report be fair, accurate and free of malice. The journalist is not so fully protected against libel action as is the legislator on the floor of the House.

Generally, however, the journalist is free to report on official, legislative and judicial proceedings without fear of successful libel action.

It is important that you know how your state defines official and public proceedings. Some states seal records in marital disputes. If you come upon or are given such a record and somehow feel compelled to publish it, you do so at your own risk. You have not only published a potential libel, but you have also broken state law.

Some occasions that look "official" and "public" are not. For example, a convention of a private organization—including a political party—is not privileged. Statements made on the floor or from the platform may not be privileged.

Publishing a story about a libel suit is a little touchy. How much detail can be safely published without repeating and extending the libel? Most of the time it is safe enough to restrict your story to details of the complaint filed with the court. However, some states do not permit the publication of contents of legal papers until there has been some judicial action.

Comment and opinion—such as criticism of a play or book—are covered by the concept of "fair comment." Provided the criticism is fair and honest and free of malice, it is protected from libel acton.

Recent U.S. Supreme Court decisions in libel appeals seem to be running more in favor of the press than they have in the last decade or so. Beginning with *New York Times* v. *Sullivan* in 1964, the "public figure" defense has been a useful tool in defeating libel actions. That decision says public figures cannot recover damages for a report related to official duties unless they can prove actual malice. Actual malice means that at the time of the publication, those responsible for the story knew it was false or published with "reckless disregard" as to whether it was true or not.

This means that a publication is to be free of damages if it is honest in its treatment of a public figure, even if some of the information it published is wrong.

Determining just who is a public figure can be difficult. Clearly, elected and appointed public officials fall in the category of "public figures." That designation has been extended to include actors, professional athletes and, yes, even TV anchorpersons. The difficulty emerges when a private person becomes involved in an event of public interest. He or she does not, by virtue of that involvement alone, become a public figure.

The courts have said in a series of decisions through the 1970s that a public figure is a person who has sought public attention—has forced him or herself into the limelight. A person forced unwillingly into public attention does not therefore become a public figure. Even involvement in a spectacular crime does not necessarily make the criminal a public figure.

Furthermore, a person once in the public eye is not necessarily a public figure forever. A child prodigy, for instance, who may have drawn great attention at the age of nine, but who has lived as a recluse for the past 20 years, probably could no longer be treated as a public figure.

A number of states have enacted so-called "negligence" standards for libel cases. Under these standards, a plaintiff need prove only that a publication was negligent in its reporting on an individual, not necessarily reckless. That is a much narrower idea and probably easier to prove.

Lower courts, where libel cases are very often tried before juries, have recently allowed huge damages. Libel judgments in excess of one-million-dollars are not uncommon. Most of them are either considerably reduced or overturned on appeal, but it is still a fearsome thing to face. Not many smaller newspapers or broadcast stations could withstand the financial impact of such a judgment.

Privacy

There is no "right" of privacy as there is a "right" of free speech. It is an evolving concept probably begun by Justice Brandeis early in this century when he spoke of a "...right to be left alone." My friend and colleague, Dr. Louis W. Hodges of Washington and Lee University, has developed a concept of "circles of intimacy;" concentric rings around ourselves each one denoting a different level of privacy, with the innermost ring that of self, where no one else gets in, to the outermost, which is the public information that is available about all of us. He says we feel "invaded" when too many people are able to enter rings we prefer to keep closed. That is probably a valuable way of looking at the problem of privacy.

Legally, when a person becomes involved in a news event, willingly or not, he or she no longer has a claim to total privacy. Ethically, however, this is a matter of serious concern. News pictures, whether on television or in print, evoke powerful emotions and some of those pictures are guaranteed to bring protests of invasion of privacy. Is it, for instance, an invasion of privacy merely to *take* a picture of someone who doesn't want the picture taken, or does the invasion not occur until the picture is actually *published*?

There is no shortage of cases where subjects of news stories or pictures believe they have been invaded.

Generally, courts have held that a person involved in a legitimate news event—as a participant or as a spectator, has lost the right of privacy as long as the photo does not single the person out for non-news reasons.

Courts have been very sympathetic toward those who claim invasion of their privacy. Judgments are not huge as they are in some libel cases, however.

As in libel, the concept of private figure versus public figure comes into play in privacy cases. Public figures have far less claim to privacy than do private figures. The President of the United States probably has almost no claim to privacy, except in the most intimate details of private life. The way a president parts his hair became "news" during one recent administration. The First Lady's taste in decorating the White House is "news."

Matters of privacy are areas where a developing body of ethical thinking applies appropriately. That is the idea that added to all the other elements of news: timeliness, proximity, consequence and all the others, should be compassion. It is believed that journalism has evolved, technologically and professionally, beyond the days of The Front Page. We are now so well-equipped to invade almost anyone's privacy, that we need to give compassionate thought to what we are doing to the subjects of our stories. It is the practice in most newsrooms not to reveal the names of rape victims. What does one do when the rapist is the victim's father? Do we publish the name and address of a mugging victim, giving potential muggers the run-down on an easy mark?

Often, we tread on privacy in feature stories where in an effort to be entertaining we inadvertently embarrass someone taking part in what he or she believed was a private event. The poor fellow trying to learn to water ski, for example, looks ridiculous. It makes marvelous video tape, however, and the temptation to shoot it is great. If the yet-to-be skier is identifiable, he probably has a privacy case.

It seems that the matter of privacy will continue to evolve over the remainder of this century. I believe we can expect the courts to begin to define the issues more clearly than they so far have.

Journalists, I believe, must become more sensitive to the issue of privacy and to the feelings of the people we routinely have covered in a somewhat offhand way. Barring that increasing sensitivity, we are going to find more and more courts happily going after the media in sympathy with offended news subjects.

Free Press-Fair Trial

The problem of maintaining a free press and fair trial procedures stems from a perceived tension between the First Amendment to the U.S. Constitution and its Sixth Amendment.

First Amendment

"Congress shall make no law respecting an establishment of religion, or prohibiting the free exercise thereof; or abridging the freedom of speech, or of the press; or the right of the people peaceably to assemble, and to petition the Government for a redress of grievances."

Sixth Amendment

"In all criminal prosecutions, the accused shall enjoy the right to a speedy and public trial, by an impartial jury of the State and district wherein the crime shall have been committed, which district shall have been previously ascertained by law, and to be informed of the nature and cause of the accusation; to be confronted with the witnesses against him; to have compulsory process for obtaining witnesses in his favor, and to have the Assistance of Counsel for his defence."

If the press is to be free to report all matters of public interest, then it seems to follow that all matters relating to criminal prosecutions must be open for publication. However, also a matter of public interest is the assurance that justice is unimpaired, especially in matters of judicial fairness. Most serious journalists will agree there are times when a free press must give way to assure an individual's liberty is not unfairly taken from him. That is why these guidelines were developed. They are not always followed precisely by either the press or the courts. Still, we Virginia journalists believe they are a valuable statement of principle and, at the very least, show there is an area in this controversy where reasonable persons can agree in the interests of both free press and fair trial.

Virginia Voluntary Guidelines*

The following is presented as representative of similar free press-fair trial guidelines in many states—not as a model. The Virginia voluntary guidelines have been in place since 1970, with some modifications over the years. Prior to 1970, problems arose in regard to news coverage of court cases, particularly in criminal cases where the rights of the defendant to an unbiased jury were seen to be jeopardized by pre-trial publicity. A 10-member committee of members of the State Bar of Virginia and the news media developed the guidelines which follow.

Principles

1. We respect the co-equal rights of a free press and a fair trial.

2. The public is entitled to as much information as possible about the administration of justice to the extent that such information does not impair the ends of justice or the rights of citizens as individuals.

3. Accused persons are entitled to be judged in an atmosphere free from passion, prejudice, and sensationalism.

4. The responsibility for assuring a fair trial rests primarily with the judge who has the power to preserve order in the court and the duty to use all means available to him to see that justice is done. All news media are equally responsible for objectivity and accuracy.

5. Decisions about handling the news rest with editors and news directors, but in the exercise of news judgments based on the public's interest the editor or news director should remember that:

* "Free Press-Fair Trial." *News Handbook on Virginia Law and Courts* 6, Richmond: The Virginia State Bar, 1984.

(a) an accused person is presumed innocent until found guilty;

(b) readers, listeners, and viewers are potential jurors;

(c) no person's reputation should be injured needlessly.

6. No lawyer should exploit any medium of public information to enhance his side of a pending case, but this should not be construed as limiting the public prosecutor's obligation to make available information to which the public is entitled.

7. The media, the bar, and law enforcement agencies should cooperate in assuring a free flow of information but should exercise responsibility and discretion when it appears probable that public disclosure of information in prosecutions might prevent a fair trial or jeopardize justice, especially just before trial.

Guidelines

To assist in decisions on the release of information, in accord with the above principles, these guidelines are recommended:

1. The following information generally should be made available for publication at or immediately after an arrest:

(a) The accused's name, age, residence, employment, family status and other factual background information.

(b) The substance or text of the charge, such as a complaint, indictment, or information and, where appropriate, the identity of the complainant and/or victim.

(c) The identity of the investigating and arresting agency or officer and the length of the investigation.

(d) The circumstances of arrest, including the time and place of arrest, resistance, pursuit, possession and use of weapons, and a description of items seized.

(e) If appropriate, the fact that the accused denies the charge.

2. The release of photographs or the taking of photographs of the accused at or immediately after an arrest should not necessarily be restricted by defense attorneys.

3. If an arrest has not been made, it is proper to disclose such information as may be necessary to enlist public assistance in apprehending fugitives from justice. Such information may include photographs, descriptions, and other factual background information including records of prior arrests and convictions. However, care should be exercised not to publish information which might be prejudicial at a possible trial.

4. The release and publication of certain types of information may tend to be prejudicial without serving a significant function of law enforcement or public interest. Therefore, all concerned should weigh carefully against pertinent circumstances the pre-trial disclosure of the following information, which normally is prejudicial to the rights of the accused:

    (a) Statements as to the character or reputation of an accused person or a prospective witness.

    (b) Admissions, confessions or the contents of a statement or alibis attributable to the accused, or his refusal to make a statement, except his denial of the charge.

    (c) The performance or results of examinations or tests or the refusal or failure of an accused to take such an examination or test.*

    (d) Statements concerning the credibility or anticipated testimony of prospective witnesses.

    (e) The possibility of a plea of guilty to the offense charged or to a lesser offense, or other disposition.

    (f) Opinions concerning evidence or argument in the case. Whether or not it is anticipated that such evidence or argument will be used at trial.

    (g) Prior criminal charges and convictions although they are usually matters of public record. Their publication may be particularly prejudicial just before trial.

5. When a trial has begun, the news media may report anything done or said in open court. The media should consider very carefully, however, publication of any

---

* It has become routine to report that a person accused of drunken driving refused to submit to blood-alcohol test.

matter or statements excluded from evidence outside the presence of the jury because this type of information is highly prejudicial and, if it reaches the jury, could result in a mistrial.

6. Law enforcement and court personnel should not encourage or discourage the photographing or televising of defendants in public places outside the courtroom.

There is an emerging body of case law that is establishing a "right of privacy" as regards the release and publication of information in criminal and civil cases. In addition, restrictions on press converage of such cases varies widely from state-to-state. As a broadcast journalist, it is your responsibility to know the practices, laws and guidelines in your state. The guidelines above, you must realize, apply only to Virginia. Furthermore, they are guidelines only, and do not have the force of law.

REFERENCES

Brandeis, Louis, and Samuel Warren. "The Right to Privacy." *Harvard Law Review* 4 (1890): 193.

Hawley, S. Edward. "Society of Professional Journalists/Sigma Delta Chi Code of Ethics." *1985–1986 Journalism Ethics Report.* Chicago: Society of Professional Journalists/Sigma Delta Chi, 1985.

Freeman, Morton. *A Treasury for Word Lovers.* Philadelphia: ISI Press, 1983.

French, Christopher W., Eileen Alt Powell, and Howard Angione, eds. *The Associated Press Stylebook and Libel Manual.* New York: The Associated Press, 1985.

"Code of Ethics." *This is Your Radio-Television News Directors Association.* Washington, D.C.: Radio-Television News Directors Association, 1966.

Hecht, Ben, and Charles MacArthur. *The Front Page.* New York: Samuel French, 1955

Hodges, Dr. Louis W. "The Journalist and Privacy." In *Social Responsibility: Journalism, Law, Medicine* (1983).

Hood, James R., and Brad Kalbfeld, eds. *The AP Broadcast News Handbook.* New York: The Associated Press, 1982.

Kilpatrick, James J. *The Writer's Art.* Kansas City: Andrews, McMeel and Parker, 1984.

Morris, William, and Mary Morris. *Harper Dictionary of Contemporary Usage.* New York: Harper and Row, 1975.

Rawson, Hugh. *A Dictionary of Euphemisms and Other Doubletalk.* New York: Crown, 1981.

Shaw, Harry. *Dictionary of Problem Words and Expressions.* New York: McGraw Hill, 1975.

Society of Professional Journalists/Sigma Delta Chi. Chicago, 1984.

The Virginia State Bar. "Free Press-Fair Trial." Section 5 of *News Handbook on Virginia Law and Courts* 6. Richmond, 1984.

Webster's Ninth New Collegiate Dictionary. Springfield, Mass.: Merriam-Webster Inc., 1985.

INDEX